THE CREATIVE GUIDE TO Crochet

PAULINE TURNER

UNWIN HYMAN

First published in Great Britain by Unwin Hyman, an imprint of Unwin Hyman Limited, 1987.

© Pauline Turner

UNWIN HYMAN LIMITED
Denmark House, 37–39 Queen Elizabeth Street, London SE1 2QB

and

40 Museum Street, London WC1A 1LU

Allen & Unwin Australia Pty Ltd
8 Napier Street, North Sydney, NSW 2060, Australia

Allen & Unwin New Zealand Pty Ltd with the Port Nicholson Press
60 Cambridge Terrace, Wellington, New Zealand

British Library Cataloguing in Publication Data.
Pauline Turner
The WI creative guide to crochet
1. Crocheting
I. Title I. National Federation of Women's Institutes
     746.43'4 TT820

ISBN 0 04 440063 2

Designed by Colin Lewis and Associates
Typeset by Latimer Trend & Company Ltd, Plymouth
Printed in Portugal by
Printer Portuguesa, Sintra

CONTENTS

INTRODUCTION

FOR MANY YEARS the word crochet has conjured up images of old lace, shawls, and ladies sitting in rocking chairs working it. In addition it often has a reputation for being ten to fifteen years 'out-of-fashion'. The projects in this book will give lie to these assumptions. Crochet can be exciting, different and most of all it is versatile. Whether you are a complete beginner or an experienced crochet worker, the pages of this book will have something stimulating and challenging for you.

To encourage newcomers to the art of crochet the book has been divided into five sections. This is possibly taking a slight risk, as what one person finds easy another will find difficult. However the patterns have been put in a progressive order so that those new to the craft can learn something about crochet with the help of simple stitches, uncomplicated shapes and easy-to-work yarn. This does not mean that the earlier patterns are stereotyped, 'old-hat', or in any way mundane, it simply means they are easy-to-follow. Written in a way that is more explanatory than usual for crochet patterns, this section includes the kind of information that will encourage better crochet. For greater detail on the crochet used throughout the book, refer to the final section on techniques.

As you work through this book from the beginning, you will discover that each pattern has suggestions for alternative ways of producing it and for different articles based on the same design.

By the end of the final section the crochet worker will have achieved a reasonably competent standard of crochet. The Landscape Waistcoat will look like a scene, fit the wearer well, and have each stitch lying flat! Hopefully, you will also find techniques or pieces of information which will help you not only to follow these projects with confidence, but which will also give you enough insight and confidence to work out a simple pattern for yourself.

It it up to you to master the art of crochet but it is hoped that it has been made as pleasurable as possible. The only criterion you need is an open mind. Have fun with your crochet and enjoy the finished product, whatever its purpose and wherever it is going.

ABBREVIATIONS WITH INTERNATIONAL SYMBOLS

backward raised treble	RtrB	Picot	p
between	bet	quadruple treble	quad tr
chain	ch	quintruple treble	quin tr
cluster	cl	raised treble	Rtr
crab stitch	cr st	repeat	rep
decrease	dec	right hand	RH
double crochet	dc	right side	RS
double knit	DK	round	rnd
double treble	dtr	second contrast	2nd C
first contrast	1st C	slip stitch	ss
forward raised treble	RtrF	space	sp
four treble cluster	4trcl	stitch	st
group	gr	three treble cluster	3trcl
half treble	htr	together	tog
increase	inc	treble	tr
left hand	LH	triple treble	tr tr
loop	lp	wrong side	WS
main shade	MS	yarn over hook	yoh
pattern	patt		

HOOK SIZES

INTERNATIONAL STANDARD RANGE (ISR)	UNITED KINGDOM		UNITED STATES	
	Wool	Cotton (Old Nos)	Wool	Cotton
10.00mm				
9.00mm	000		15	
	00		13	
8.00mm	0		12	
	1		11	
7.00mm	2		$10\frac{1}{2}$ K	
	3		10 J	
6.00mm	4		9 I	
5.50mm	5		8 H	
5.00mm	6		7	
4.50mm	7		6 G	
4.00mm	8		5 F	
3.50mm	9		4 E	
			3 D	
3.00mm	10	3/0	2 C	
	11	2/0		0
2.50mm	12	0	1 B	1
	13	1	0	2
				3
2.00mm	14	$1\frac{1}{2}$		4
		2		5
1.75mm		$2\frac{1}{2}$		6
		3		
1.50mm		$3\frac{1}{2}$		7
		4		8
1.25mm		$4\frac{1}{2}$		9
		5		10
1.00mm		$5\frac{1}{2}$		11
		6		12
0.75mm		$6\frac{1}{2}$		13
0.60mm		7		14
		$7\frac{1}{2}$		
		8		

P A R T   O N E
Easy

IN THE PINK

See page 10

Most newcomers to crochet want to make something that can be worn. Many commercial patterns are limited by space and this need for brevity in writing crochet patterns, is frequently off-putting to beginners. Similarly, the patterns that are not too difficult to work, are often designed for fluffy or textured yarn which absolute beginners find difficult to handle. This type of yarn pulls against the fingers making an even tension harder to achieve. In addition, it is not easy to know where to insert the hook in very fluffy yarn.

Garments should fit well if the worker is to feel satisfied which means some shaping is necessary. As decreasing in crochet is more complicated than increasing, the very easy-to-make, easy-to-wear waistcoat below is shaped by increasing only.

Materials: 400g (450g: 450g: 500g) Forsell Slalom Pure Wool Aran 6.00mm hook.

Size: 80–86 (88–96: 97–102: 106–112)cm
  32–34 (34½–37½: 38–40: 42–44)in
Back length: 61cm (24in)
Side seam: 35cm (10½in)

Tension:
6sts and 3 rows to 5cm (2in) over trebles on the 6.00mm hook.

TO MAKE
Make 49 (55:60:66)ch loosely as this is at hip level.
Row 1: 1tr in 4th ch from hook do not count loop on hook, 1tr in each ch to end, 3ch, turn (47(53:58:64)sts).

Note: the 3ch made at the end of the row is the first st of the next row.
Row 2: 1tr in each st to end, 3ch, turn.
Repeat row 2, 32 times, (35 rows in all).
Divide work for fronts at shoulders as follows:
Row 36: 1tr in next 14 (17:18:20)sts (turning ch has already been worked)
3ch, turn, (25(18:19:21)sts).
Row 37: As row 2. Repeat row 2, 6 times.
Row 44: 1tr in next 13(16:17:19)sts, 2tr in last st, 3ch, turn.
16(19:20:22)sts. This gives an increase on the front edge.
Work row 2, 3 times.
Row 48: 1tr in each st until last st remains, 2tr in last st, 3ch, turn.
Work row 2, 3 times.
Repeat the last 4 rows (that is inc row plus 3 plain rows) twice, 19(22:23:25)sts.
Work row 48 once. 20(23:24:26)sts.
Work row 2, 15 times. Break off yarn.
Connect yarn at neck edge (not side edge) to work other front.
To do this miss 17(17:20:22)sts, and join into 18th (18th:21st:23rd)st, 3ch, tr to end, 3ch, turn, (17(18:19:21)sts). Work row 2, 7 times more on these 15(18:19:21)sts.
Row 44(a): 1tr in same place as turning ch (that is the hole that is usually missed) which acts as an increase, 1tr in each st to end, 3ch, turn, (16(19:20:22)sts).
Work 3 rows as row 2.
Repeat the last 4 rows 3 times.
Work row 44(a) once, (20(23:24:26)sts).
Work row 2, 15 times.
Break off yarn.
Note: This work does NOT need pressing.

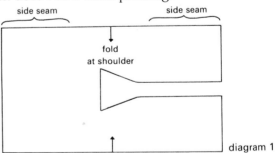

diagram 1

See diagram 1. Shape of work.
There is no right and wrong side to crochet at this stage.
Place the best side inside and using safety pins, pin the side seams by folding fronts to match base of back. It should be level with the sides and base corners. Double crochet the bottom 18 rows together to form the side seam. Use 3dc for every 2 treble row ends.
Break off yarn.
Join other side to match.
Front and Base Borders
With right side facing, rejoin yarn into centre stitch at back neck,

1ch, 7(7,8,9)dc, dec 1st at corner by working last neck st and first front side st tog, work 3dc to 2tr row ends as before, down front (58sts) includng ½st at neck, 2dc in corner, 1dc in each st at base of waistcoat to next front. There is only 1 strand to pick up at back base edge, 2dc in corner, 57dc up front, 1dc at corner, 7(7,9,10)dc, join at centre with a ss. 1ch, TURN—very important.

Row 2: dc to bottom front corner, 3dc in corner, dc along base, 3dc in corner, dc up front and round neck to centre back, join with ss, 1ch, turn.

Row 3: dc to neck corner, dec 1st round neck and front, dc to corner, 2dc in corner, dc across base, 2dc in corner, dc up front, dec 1st at back corner, dc to centre back, join with ss, 1ch, turn.

Row 4: Work row 2 once.

Ideally with right side facing, work 1 row crab stitch or simply work another row of dc as row 3.

Armhole Border

Having broken off yarn from previous border, rejoin to underarm seam with wrong side facing. Work 22dc over next 14 rows as described before, put 1dc in each of next 8tr row ends as this pulls the shoulder onto the arm for a better fit, 22dc in remaining 14 rows, join with ss, 1ch, TURN.

Row 2: 1dc in each st to shoulder, dec 1st over 2 shoulder, 1dc in each st to end, join with ss. Do not turn work as right side is facing. Crab stitch round armhole, miss 2sts evenly at shoulder point. Join with ss.

Break off yarn.

Work another armhole to match.

Break the remainder of the yarn into 4 even lengths and using the 4 lengths as one strand, crochet a sufficiently long chain to thread through the trebles of the waistcoat at your waist level. By crocheting the 4 strands together a rope-like tie is made.

Secure both ends very carefully.

PEACH SORBET

See page 11

This design is primarily for those people who want to learn how to crochet Victorian 'lace' patterns. Although the simple cotton top pattern given below has been classified as suitable for beginners, it must be pointed out that cotton, particularly mercerized cotton, does not have any 'give'. Should the tension be very wrong, or the stitches uneven, it will show in the garment.

The design of the top is such that it will fit most sizes even if

the finished garment is a little larger or smaller than stated. The style looks feminine if it clings to the body, and fashionable if it hangs loosely so either way you succeed. Underarm shaping has not been included as there is no shaping involved, it is simply made up of 2 rectangles. However, the network of stitches on the yoke gives an illusion of shaping as the yoke finds its own level.

Materials: 3 balls Tootal Cotton (80g): 3.00mm crochet hook.

Size: To fit bust size 80 (90:100)cm (32(35:38)in)

Tension: 25sts to 10cm (4in) worked with 3.00mm hook over trebles.

TO MAKE:
With 3.00mm hook make 102 (114:126)ch.
Do not count loop on hook.
Row 1: ltr in 4th ch from hook, this makes your first 2 stitches, ltr in each ch to end, 3ch, turn (100(112:124)sts).

Helpful hint: It is a good idea to count your stitches regularly. If you keep losing or making stitches, it is helpful to put a small safety pin in every 25th stitch and count between the pins, rather than work the whole row only to discover you missed or made a stitch 90sts ago!
Row 2: tr to end, that is tr in each st inserting hook under 2 strands at top of stitch below, 3ch, turn.
Work this row 45 times more (35cm(14in)).

Yoke
Row 1: *5ch, miss 2sts, 1dc in next st, rep from * to end, 5ch, turn, (33(38:42) loops).
Row 2: 1dc in first loop, *5ch, 1dc in next loop, rep from * to end, 3ch, 1dc in same loop, turn.

Helpful hint: Work dc in the space, not in a chain. This helps to keep the tension more even. Once the yoke is completed ease the dc along the chain to form even spaces.

Row 3: *5ch, 1dc in loop, rep from * to end.
Repeat rows 2 and 3, 9 times.
Fasten off.
Make another piece the same.
Join side seams, (that is the treble rows).
Join shoulders by (a) oversewing each pair of loops together in the centre to form a diamond. OR (b) attach the yarn to the centre chain of one of the loops at the armhole edge, 3ch, 1dc in centre of matching loop on other piece, *3ch, 1dc in next loop of other piece, rep from * until all shoulder loops have been worked into on both pieces. Work other shoulder to match.

Helpful hint: Do not make neck opening too small as it is designed to be a slashed neck.

Possible finishing touches

Work 5ch, 1dc into every loop round armholes.
Edge base of garment with (5ch, miss 2sts, 1dc in next st) until all the stitches have been used.

TREBLE VARIATION CUSHIONS

See page 14

The pattern for the neat two-coloured rectangular cushion is 'V' stitch. This is a simple variation using only trebles (with turning and foundation chain of course). By inserting the hook in the SPACE lying between the two trebles that make a group, the hook pushes the trebles sideways at the top, creating a 'V' shape.

Absolute Beginners to Crochet

Break off the yarn at the end of every row. At the same time turn on every row. This method unfortunately leaves numerous ends which require darning in. It is worth trying the method of turning as described below.

Turning work after 2 rows

It is not necessary to turn crochet on every row. In this pattern one row of 'V' stitch is in colour 'A', the next row in colour 'B', throughout the cushion. To save breaking off the yarns at each end, the pattern is written in a way which turns the work after BOTH colours have been used (that is after two rows have been worked).

Changing colours

To avoid a 'colour drag' DO NOT complete the last stitch of the row. Instead, work the last stitch until two loops remain on the hook. Complete the stitch with the new colour.

Cushion pads

The cushion pads should be larger than the cushion cover. This prevents the cover wrinkling and looking baggy, as a good cushion should look plump and inviting but with a 'soft-to-the-touch' finish.

Weights (for neck cushion)

These can be small flat stones that have been washed and covered,

Detail of cushion, the contrasting 'V' effect is composed of trebles.

14

Detail of textured blanket, this simple stitch forms the foundation for the rug.

Detail of the pram rug, the Surface Crochet Chain is accentuated by using contrasting wools.

small pieces of metal, marbles, or even coins. These are required to counter-balance the weight of the cushion cover and the cushion pad. If too much weight is included the cushion will constantly fall to the ground. Conversely, if insufficient weight is included the neck cushion will end up as a scatter cushion with tails.

RECTANGULAR SCATTER CUSHION

Materials: 2 × 50g Main colour Sirdar 2 × 50g Contrast 4.50mm hook and 3.50mm hook for neck cushion

Size: 45 × 30cm (18 × 12in)

Tension: 8sts (4'V'sts) to 6cm (2$\frac{1}{4}$in)

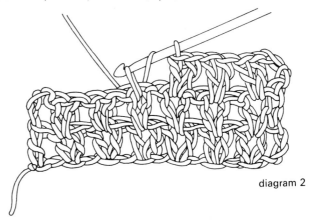

diagram 2

TO MAKE
With 4.50mm hook and Contrast make 63ch.
Row 1: 2tr in 5th ch from hook * miss 1ch, 2tr in next ch, rep from * until 2ch remain, 1tr in last ch. Change to Main 3ch, turn.
Row 2: *2tr in space between the 2tr of row below (see diagram 2) rep from * to last st, 1tr in last st. Change to Contrast, 3ch, turn.
Row 3: 2tr in centre of 2tr of row below, rep from * to last st, 1tr in last st, change to Main, 3ch, turn.
Rep rows 2 and 3, 10 times.
Fasten off.
Make another piece the same.

With wrong sides together and using Main, double crochet the two pieces on the RS by working 1dc in Main stripe and 2 rows dc in Contrast stripe.
Place 2dc at corners with 1dc in every st along top and bottom edges. Before the 4th side is closed insert the cushion pad. Join with ss.
Final row: Crab stitch all round. Fasten off.

RECTANGULAR NECK CUSHION
Make scatter cushion as given with Main and 3.50mm hook, fold back the border joining the 2 sides of the cushion together. Connect into 7th st, 1ch, 3dc, 1ch, turn.

Next row: dc to end, 1ch, turn.
Continue working rows of dc 30cm (12in). Fold back the last 5cm (2in) and sew in a weight.
Make a corresponding strap at the other end.

TEXTURED BLANKET AND RUG

See page 15

As pointed out in the Introduction there are designs for each level of crochet skill. The pattern for the pram blanket is easy-to-make. However, all good baby designs have to make allowance for the smallness of baby fingers. As a blanket (between a sheet and top cover) this design provides insulation.

Using the open fabric as a base, the blanket can be converted into a rug at a higher level of skill.

BLANKET

Materials: 150g Forsell Slalom Pure Wool Aran: 4.50mm and 5.50mm crochet hooks

Size: 45cm × 50cm (see note below blanket)

Tension: 12sts (6sps) to 9cm ($3\frac{3}{4}$in)

TO MAKE:
With 5.50mm hook make 61ch (Do not count loop on hook).
Row 1: Keeping the smooth side of the chain facing for easier working, make 1tr in 5th ch from hook *miss 1ch, make 1ch, (to replace stitch missed) 1tr in next ch, repeat from * to end. This gives you 30sps, 4ch, (3ch are for the tr st that keeps the sides straight and 1ch is for the first sp) turn.
Row 2: *1tr in next tr (that is picking up 2 strands of treble and not going into the space), 1ch, rep from * to end, 4ch, turn.
Repeat row 2, 35 times.
Fasten off.
A row of dc can be made to neaten the edges if wished.
With 5.50mm hook work 1dc in each st at top edge; change to a 4.50mm hook and put 2dc in each row down side: change to 5.50mm hook and picking up the single strand left from the foundation ch dc across base; change to 4.50mm hook and work as for otherside.

Note: It is necessary to put 3dc in each corner to keep the right angle point.

(Note: to make a larger blanket add more chain but the total must alway amount to an odd number, then work more rows to keep the proportion.)

PRAM RUG

Materials: 150g Forsell Slalom Pure Wool Aran: 100g Contrast: 4.50mm, 5.50mm and 10.00mm crochet hooks

Size and Tension: as for the blanket.

TO MAKE
Work a base as given for the blanket.
Using the 10.00mm hook and extra yarn work rows of surface crochet chain as given below.

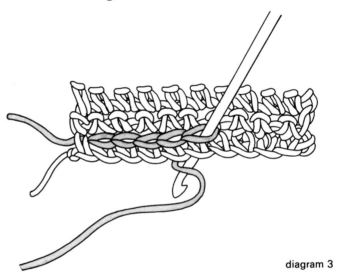

diagram 3

Surface Crochet Chain
Have yarn always beneath the blanket and the hook above the blanket. See diagram 3. Use 2 strands of contrast together.
Work 1ch in each hole to end of row. *Make 1 extra chain to take the yarn from 1 row to the next. Bend this chain round and keeping the yarn below the blanket continue placing 1ch in each hole to end. Repeat from * until all the blanket is covered. Break off yarn.
Darn in ends carefully to make sure they will not come undone or spoil the stitch pattern.

BORDERS AND BUTTONS

See page 22.

The pattern for this jacket uses the same principle as the waistcoat to avoid decreasing. That is, the fronts continue down from the shoulders. The sleeves have been worked up from the cuff edge.

Materials: 500(550,600,650)g Sirdar in Main: 50g in Contrast: 4.50mm crochet hook: 8 buttons (or 3.50mm hook if making own buttons)

Size: 80–86(88–96: 97–102: 106–112)cm
(32–34(34$\frac{1}{2}$–37$\frac{1}{2}$: 38–40: 42–44)in)
Back length: 61cm (24in) Underarm sleeve seam: 45cm (17$\frac{1}{2}$in)

Tension: 8sts to 5cm (2in) 8 rows to 9cm (3$\frac{1}{2}$in)

TO MAKE:

Back
With 4.50mm hook and Main yarn make 74(82:88:96)ch. (Do not count loop on hook).
Row 1: 1tr in 4th ch from hook, 1tr in each ch to end, 3ch, turn. (72(80:86:94)sts)
Row 2: 1tr in each st to end, 3ch, turn.
Work row 2, 49 times more (57cm(22$\frac{1}{2}$in)).
Note: If you have to alter the number of rows because your tension is not the same as that given, do so in multiples of 5 so that the front can be adjusted by 1 row between the buttonholes.

Left Front
This is worked from the shoulder down as a continuation of the back.
Row 1: 19(22,24,28)tr (the 3ch should have been worked already for the first st), 3ch, turn (20(23,25,29)sts)
Row 2: tr to end, 3ch, turn
Repeat row 2, 14 times.
Row 17: tr to last st, 2tr in last st, 3ch, turn (21(24,26,30)sts).
Work row 2, 3 times.
Work row 17 once (22(25,27,31)sts).
Repeat the last 4 rows 4 times (26(29,31,35)sts).
Work row 2, 26 times.
Fasten off.

Right side
Rejoin yarn to the neck side of the back by leaving 24(36,38,38)sts unworked.
Row 1: 3ch, 1tr in each remaining st, 3ch, turn (29(23,25,29)sts).

Row 2: tr to end, 3ch, turn.
Repeat row 2 twice.
Row 5: tr to end, 38(40,42,42)ch.
Row 6: 1tr in 4th ch from hook, 1tr in each ch and 1tr in each st to end, 3ch, turn (56(61,65,69)sts).
Row 7: tr to end, 3ch, turn.
Row 8: 1tr, miss 1st, 1ch (in place of st and to make the buttonhole) tr to end, 3ch, turn.
Row 9: tr to end, putting 1tr in each st and in the space created by the ch, 3ch, turn.
Work row 7, 7 times.
Row 15: tr to last 3sts, 1st, 1ch, 2tr, 3ch, turn.
Row 16: As row 9.
Work row 7, 7 times.
Work rows 8–25 twice.
Now work rows 8 and 9 once.
Fasten off.

Sleeves (2 alike)
With 4.50mm hook and Main yarn make 58ch.
Row 1: 1tr in 4th ch from hook, 1tr in each ch to end, 3ch, turn (56sts).
Row 2: tr to end, 3ch, turn.
Repeat row 2, 6 times.
Row 9: 1tr in same place as turning ch (increasing 1st), tr to last st, 2tr in last st, 3ch, turn (58sts).
Row 10: As row 2.
Repeat rows 9 and 10, 13 times (84sts).
Work row 2 twice.
Fasten off.

Cuffs
Row 1: Rejoin Main yarn to foundation row. There will be only one strand. With 4.50mm hook make 1ch, 1dc in each stitch to end, 1ch, turn.
Row 2: dc to end. Change to Contrast before working one turning chain. Fasten off Main.
Row 3: In Contrast work 1 row dc.
Row 4: RS facing (if necessary mark with a safety pin) crab st to end. Fasten off.
Note: beginners to crochet can work row 4 as dc if wished.

Fold jacket at shoulders so that the base of the back and fronts are level. The fold should connect with the centre of the sleeve. Safety pin the sleeves into place making sure they match exactly. Join by either double crocheting on the wrong side or by sewing. Join underarm seams of sleeve and side seam of jacket all in one.

Border
With 4.50mm hook, RS facing, and Main yarn, join to centre st at back neck. 1ch, dc to corner; dc down left front by putting 3dc to each 2 rows inserting hook through the stitches (not in the spaces);

put 2dc at corner; 1dc in each foundation chain to right front; 2dc in corner; dc up right front putting 3dc to each 2 row ends; 2dc at right angled corner of neck, 1dc in each st across neck; dc over shoulder putting 3dc in 2 row ends, dc to centre back, join with ss.

Row 2: 1ch, *TURN*, put 1dc in each st to front corner of neck, 2dc in corner, dc down right front, 2dc in corner, dc across base, 2dc at corner, dc to back neck, join with ss. Break off Main yarn.

Row 3: Join in Contrast, 1ch, dc all round placing 2dc at corner points, join with ss.

Row 4: With RS facing crab st all the way round. Join with ss. Fasten off.

Buttons make 8

With 3.50mm hook and Main, make the slip knot to slide from the tail end of the yarn (if this cannot be achieved work 3ch, join into a ring with ss) 3ch, into first ch work 7htr, join with ss. Fasten off. Tighten central hole by pulling the tail end. Join in Contrast 1ch, *1dc worked loosely through centre of button, 1dc, rep from * 3 times, join with ss. 1ch, dc to end. Leave a long end. Fill case with an old button or toy filling (or the yarn used for the jacket). Use end to gather casing tightly over middle.

PART TWO

Moderately Easy

BABY'S RABBIT BAG

See page 26

Ideal for a restless baby! Any motif can be crocheted and then appliqued to the bib. Alternatively, you can buy ready-made motifs.

The number of buttonholes in the straps can be increased, or decreased depending upon the size of the baby.

Materials: 150g Sirdar Chunky: 5.50mm and 7.00mm hook: 4 Rabbit buttons: plus 25g DK Contrast and 4.50mm hook (optional).

Size: To fit up to 9 months.

Tension: 5sts to 6 rows (2in)

TO MAKE:
With 7.00mm hook and chunky yarn make 31ch.
Row 1: 1dc into 3rd ch from hook, 1dc in each st to end, 1ch, turn.
Row 2: 1dc in each st to end, 1ch, turn.
Note: It is easy to lose a st when working dc, so CHECK that the last st (ie. the turning ch of the row below) has been worked into.
Rep row 2 until 60cm (24in) have been worked.
Do not fasten off yarn but fold beginning of rectangle up to level of work. Join to the foundation row by working 1 row dc on the wrong side.
Note: There is no wrong side of the work until the join has been completed.
Continue across folded side of rectangle joining sides together to form a bag. This gives a side seam. Fasten off. If desired the join can be placed at centre back by breaking off the yarn once the foundation ch has been attached to the work. However if the dc is not soft this could make an uncomfortable ridge for the baby.

Border
With 7.00mm hook join yarn to side seam, 1ch, 59dc round top of

bag, join with ss, 1ch, TURN work.
Note: This should work out at approximately 3dc to 4 rows of treble. Most people will work approximately 80 rows to reach 60cm.
Row 2: 1dc in each st, join with ss, 1ch, turn.
Rep row 2, twice. Fasten off yarn.

Bib

Row 1: With 7.00mm hook rejoin yarn into 9th st from side seam, 1ch, 13dc, 1ch, turn.
Row 2: dc to end, 1ch, turn.
Rep row 2 until bib measures 10cm (4in).
Fasten off.
Extra: One row crab st can be worked all round border and the 3 sides of the bib if wished, for a better finish.

Shoulder Straps

With 5.50mm hook and back of bag facing join yarn to 17th st from side of bib counting from the side away from join 1ch, 1dc in same place as ch, 1dc in next st, 2dc in next st, 1ch, turn (5sts in all).
Row 2: dc to end, 1ch, turn.
Rep row 2 until 14cm (5½in) has been worked.
*Buttonhole row: 1dc, 1ch, miss 1st, 2dc, 1ch, turn.
Next row: dc to end (placing 1dc in sp created by ch, not in the ch itself) 1ch, turn.
Work row 2 once.
●Work from * twice more (3 buttonholes worked).
Final row: dc2tog twice.
Fasten off.
Miss 14sts and work another strap to match.
Cross these straps over at back.
Sew a button at each corner of bib (see picture).

Side Straps

With RS of work facing and 5.50mm hook, pinch side seam so that the border can be worked into directly.
Join yarn to edge of border, 1ch, 4dc to beg. of border (ie. over depth) 1ch, turn.
Work 5 rows dc.
Work from * to ● up shoulder strap twice.
Work final row as shoulder strap.
Work another strap to match by pinching border into a fold that is exactly opposite to side seam to produce a mock side seam for the other side of the bag.
Sew 2 buttons on border to form a square with the 2 buttons at corner of bib (see picture).

Rabbit Motif

This is an easy, almost cheating way to make a rabbit.

Head

Using white DK yarn and 4.50mm hook make 4ch, join into a ring

to form a circle. To prevent a hole forming at the centre of this circle make 3ch and work into the first chain made. It is ESSENTIAL that the slip knot made can be tightened by pulling up the tail piece, not the ball thread—see Techniques, 11tr in centre of ring (or chain), join with ss ** 1ch turn.
Rnd 2: 2dc in each st to end.
Rnd 3: Crab st back (this is the right side row).

Ears
Rnd 4: 1ch, 1dc in next st, 1ch turn (2sts).
Rnd 5: 1dc, 1ch, turn.
Rep row 5 twice.
Break off yarn.
Miss 2sts, join in yarn and work rows 4–7 incl, once.

Body
Work as head to **.
Rnd 2: 3ch, 1tr in same place, 2tr in each st to end, join with ss.
Rnd 3: Crab st to end.

To Assemble
Slightly distort both circles into rather fat oval shapes.
Overlap the head on the body.
Place these centrally on the bib.
Make a tiny pom-pom for a tail and attach. Alternatively, make a looped tassel that is short but fat, to avoid any bits being pulled out by inquisitive figures.

SIMPLE SNOOD

See page 27
This is a combination of a pull-on hat and the new style of 'snood' (a long tube that can be pulled over the hair and tucked under the chin). The hat is simply extended to form a tube leaving a slit for the eyes. A fashionably practical article of headwear for people who have to go to town but also walk the dog on moors in the snow.

Materials: 450g in Main: 50g in Contrast Forsell Aran: 5.50mm Crochet hook

Size: To fit an average adult head

Tension: 5sts to 5cm (2in)

TO MAKE:

Using the 5.50mm crochet hook and Main yarn work 4ch, join into a ring with a slip stitch through the first of the 4ch made.

Rnd 1: 3ch, 13tr in centre of ring, join top of 3ch with a ss (14sts).

Rnd 2: With wrong side facing and Contrast yarn join into any stitch *1tr in next st, 1ss in next st, rep from * to last st 1tr in last st, join with a ss to start of Contrast yarn.

Break off this yarn.

Rnd 3: 3ch to turn *2tr in next st, rep from * to end, 1tr in same place as turning ch, join to top of turning ch with a ss (28sts).

Rnd 4: 3ch, turn *2tr in next st, 1tr in next st, rep from * to last st, 2tr in last st, join with ss to top of turning ch (42sts).

Rnd 5: 3ch to turn *2tr in next st, 2tr, rep from * to last 2sts, 2tr in next st, 1tr in last st, join to top of turning ch with ss (56sts).

Rnd 6: 3ch, turn, tr to end, ss in top of turning ch.

Work Rnd 6, 7 times more.

With wrong side of work facing join in Contrast and work as for Row 2.

Break off yarn.

Rnd 14: In Main make 1ch, dc to end.

Rnd 15: 1ch, turn, 19dc, 16ch missing 16sts, 20dc, ss to top of turning ch.

Rnd 16: 1ch turn, dc to end, ss in top of turning ch.

Rnd 17: As round 13.

Rnd 18: 3ch in Main, turn, tr to end, join with ss into top of turning ch.

Rep this round 9 times.

Rnd 28: As round 13.

Rnd 29: As round 16.

Rep the last two rounds once.

Final Rnd: Work 1 row crab stitch with right side facing.

Fasten off all ends.

See diagram 3 which shows how to fold the mouth and neck piece to form a hat.

SQUARE TABLECLOTH

See page 30

It is always neater to join a motif to its neighbour during the last round of the motif. It appears easier to make a full strip of motifs [in this case 12], joined to each other as only 1 edge of the square needs to be thought about. At this stage both the working of the motif and the joining have become familiar. Thus when the second strip of 12 motifs is being added, each motif can be joined on 2 sides without any confusion.

A picot (p) is a small space made by chains. The number of chains varies according to the pattern, and whether the picot is joined with a slip stitch or double crochet also varies from pattern to pattern. Normally the first picot worked will describe exactly what number of chain, and which method of joining is to be used in that pattern. On average, 3 chains make the actual picot and a slip stitch is then put onto the stitch from which the 3 chains have originated (see row 2).

Materials: 24 balls of Coats Chain Mercer-Crochet Cotton No. 20 (20g). 1.25mm hook.

Size: 114cm (45in) square.

Tension: Size of motif 9.5cm (3¾in) square.

TO MAKE

First Motif
Commence with 12ch.

Row 1: *3tr tr (leaving the last lp of each st on hook) into 12th ch from hook, draw through all lps on hook (cl made), 1yoh, 13ch rep from *3 times omit 12ch, at end of last rep, 1ss into same place as 1st cl.
Row 2: *12dc into next lp, 1dc into next 1chsp, 3ch, 1ss into last dc (a p made), rep from *to end 1ss in 1st dc.
Row 3: 1ss in next 2dc, * (1dc into next dc, 13ch) 5 times, 1dc into next dc, 7ch, miss 3dc p and 3dc; rep from * ending with 1ss into 1st dc.
Row 4: 1ss into each of next 5ch, 3dc into lp, *5ch, 3dc into next lp, (3ch, 3dc into next lp) twice, 5ch, 3dc into next lp, 7ch, 3dc into next 13ch lp, rep from * omitting 3dc at end of last rep, 1ss into 1st dc.
Row 5: 1ss into each of next 4sts, 1dc into lp, *(5ch, 1dc into next lp) 3 times, (8ch, 1dc into next lp) twice; rep from * omit 1dc at end of last rep, 1ss into 1st dc.
Row 6: 2ch, *(5 htr into next lp, 1htr into next dc) 3 times, (into next lp work 1dc, 1htr, 5tr, 1htr and 1dc) twice, 1htr into next dc, rep from * omit 1htr at end of last rep, 1ss into 2nd of 2ch.
Row 7: 1dc into same place as ss, *(5ch, miss 5sts, 1dc into next st) 3 times, 5ch, miss 4sts, 1dc into next st, 14ch, miss 8sts, 1dc into next st, 5ch, miss 4sts, 1dc into next st, rep from * omit 1dc at end of last rep, 1ss into first dc.
Row 8: *(into next lp work 1dc, 1htr, 3tr, 1htr and 1dc) 4 times, into next lp work 1dc 1htr 13tr 1htr and 1dc, into next lp work 1dc 1htr 3tr 1htr and 1dc; rep from * ending with 1ss into 1st dc.
Row 9: 1ss into each of next 2sts, *(into next st work 1dc 5ch and 1dc, 4ch, miss 6sts) 4 times, 1dc into each of next 5sts, into next st work 1dc 9ch and 1dc, 1dc into each of next 5sts, 4ch, miss 6sts, into next st work 1dc 5ch and 1dc, 4ch, miss 6sts, rep from * ending with 1ss into 1st dc. Fasten off.

Second Motif

Work as 1st motif for 8 rows.

Row 9: 1ss into each of next 2sts, (into next st work 1dc 5ch and 1dc, 4ch, miss 6sts) 4 times, 1dc into each of next 6sts, 4ch, 1dc into corresponding lp on 1st motif, 4ch, 1dc into same place as last dc on 2nd motif, 1dc into each of next 5sts, (4ch, miss 6sts, 1dc into next st, 2ch 1dc into next 5ch lp on 1st motif, 2ch, 1dc into same place as last dc on 2nd motif) 5 times, 4ch, miss 6sts, 1dc into each of next 6sts, 4ch, 1dc into next 9ch lp on 1st motif 4ch, 1dc into same place as last dc on 2nd motif and complete as 1st motif.

Make 12 rows of 12 motifs joining each as 2nd motif was joined to 1st. Where 4 corners meet join 3rd and 4th motifs to joining of previous motifs.

Damp and pin out to measurement.

AUBERGINE BODYWARMER

See page 31

For the active person, or one who has to stand around cheering the more energetic members of the family and friends.
Note: Shaping has been kept to a minimum but some increasing gives an interesting design line to the neck.

Materials: 500(550,600,650,700)g Forsell Aran Pure Wool: 6.00mm and 5.00mm hooks: 9 buttons

Size: To fit bust/chest 80(90,100,110,120)cm
(32(35,39,43,47)in)

Actual Size: 85(95,105,115,125)cm (34(37,41,45,49)in)

Tension: 6trs to 5cm (2in)

TO MAKE:

Body

In Main and with 6.00mm hook make 108(120,132,144,156)ch.
Row 1: 1dc in 3rd ch from hook, 3ch, turn (107)119,131,143,155)sts).
Row 2: 1tr in each st to end, 1ch, turn. Note: the 1ch is the first st.
Row 3: *1RtrF, 1dc, rep from * to end, 1ch, turn.
Row 4: *1dtr, 1dc, rep from * to end, 1ch, turn.
Row 5: dc to end, 3ch, turn.
Rep rows 2–5, 8 times.

Divide for Armholes

Left Side
On first 27(29,33,35,39)sts only (including turning chain) work rows 2–5, 5 times.
Next row: ss over 10, 3ch, tr to end, 3ch, turn (17(19,23,25,29)sts).
Work rows 3–5 once and then rows 2–5 twice. Fasten off yarn.

Back
Miss 1(2,1,2,1)st at armhole and with wrong side facing rejoin yarn to next st, 3ch, 50(56,62,68,74)tr 1ch, turn.
Work 24 rows more in pattern, (ending in a tr row). Fasten off.

Right Side
Miss 1(2, 1, 2, 1)st at armhole with wrong side facing rejoin yarn into next st, 3ch, tr to end, 3ch, turn (27(29,33,35,39)sts).
Work rows 3–5 once.
Rep patt rows 2–5, 3 times.
Next row: tr to last st, 2tr in last st, 1ch, turn.
Next row: 1dc in same place as turning ch. *1RtrF, 1dc, rep from * to end, 1ch, turn.
Next row: *1dtr, 1dc, rep from * to last st, 2dc in last st, 1ch, turn.
Next row: 1dc in same place as turning ch, dc to end, 3ch, turn.
Rep the last 4 rows once (35(37,41,43,47)sts).
Next row: 16(18,22,24,28)tr, 1ch, turn (17(19,23,25,29)sts).
Work 7 rows pattern on these 17(19,23,25,29)sts.
Break off yarn.

Armhole Border
With RS facing join yarn to underarm seam, dc round armhole (4dc to each pattern) dc2tog underarm, join with ss, 1ch, turn.
Row 2: dc2tog, dc to shoulder, dc2tog, dc to underarm, ss to join, 1ch, turn.
Rep row 2 once.
With RS facing and 5.00mm hook work 1 row crab stitch.
Fasten off.
Work another armhole to match.

Mock Pocket Flap
With 5.00mm hook work 15ch, 1dc in 3rd ch from hook, 1dc in each ch to end, 1ch, turn.
Work 3 rows dc.
With RS facing work 1 row crab stitch.
Fasten off.

Front and Neck Border
With 6.00mm hook join yarn to base of R front, dc up front to point of increase putting 4dc in each pattern; dc2tog, dc to point, 4dc in point, dc across front flap, dc2tog at shoulder, dc over shoulder, dc2tog at back neck corner, dc across back neck, dc2tog at shoulder, dc over shoulder, dc2tog at front neck, dc across neck, 3dc in corner point, dc down left front, 1ch, turn.

Row 2: dc to neck, 2dc in corner, dc all round neck to point at right front flap, 3dc in corner st, dc to end, 1ch, turn.

Row 3: Evenly mark 6 button positions on the Left side border (one button should be at start of flap increase). *dc to marker, 1ch, miss 1st (1 buttonhole made), rep from * 5 times, dc to corner, 1dc 1ch 1dc in corner, (7 buttonholes made—see photograph) dc across neck, dc2tog, dc over shoulder, dc2tog, dc across back neck, dc2tog, dc over shoulder, dc2tog, dc across neck, 3dc in corner, dc down front.

Row 4: As row 2.

Row 5: As row 1.

Row 6: With RS facing and 5.00mm hook work 1 row crab st. Complete by sewing on 8 buttons to match the 8 buttonholes.

Sew 1 button to centre of mock pocket flap.

Look at photograph to see where to attach the base and two sides of the flap to the RH side of the garment. It should lie in a horizontal line with the button on the front band.

AUTUMNAL CARDIGAN

See opposite

This is an easy-to-wear tie belt cardigan. The fronts can be extended if necessary by working the band to twice its width. This will give the neck a roll-back collar.

Materials: 400(450,500,550,600)g Main colour Forsell 4-ply pure wool: 50g Dark contrast: 50g Medium contrast: 50g Light contrast: 3.50mm and 4.50mm hooks.

Size: To fit bust/chest 82(92,102,112,122)cm
(32(36,40,44,48)in)

Tension: 5 rows and 9sts to 4cm(2in) worked over trebles on a 4.00mm hook

TO MAKE:

Worked in 1 piece from cuff to cuff.

Note: There is no right or wrong way of this crochet until folded in half. The fold should have the stripes on the right sleeve for a woman, or the left sleeve for a man.

With a 4.50mm hook and Main work 64ch.

Row 1: 1dc in 3rd ch from hook, 1dc in each ch to end. Fasten off (63sts).

Row 2: Change to Dark contrast 3ch, tr to end, 3ch, turn.

Work 4 more rows in this colour. Change to Main.

Row 7: 3ch, tr to end, fasten off Main. Join in Medium contrast.

Row 8: 3ch, tr to end.

Rep row 8, 3 times. Fasten off. Join in Main.
Row 12: Work 1 row trebles. Fasten off. Join in Light contrast.
Row 13: 3ch, tr to end.
Rep row 13 twice. Fasten off. Join in Main.
Row 16: inc 1st at beg and end of the row.
Rep row 16 twice (69sts).
Work 1 row without increasing.
Rep the last 4 rows 3 times (87sts).
Work 2 further rows increasing (91sts).
Continue until work measures 42cm 16in (or 1in less than your underarm seam)

Add Chain for Body
With yarn from another ball work 63ch from top of turning chain of row just worked.
Fasten off.
With yarn still attached work 65ch.
*Next row: 1tr in 4th ch from end, 1tr in each ch to sleeve, 1tr in each st across sleeve, 1tr in each ch to end, 3ch turn (217sts).
This piece of crochet goes over the front and down the back of the garment in one strip. The stripes over the shoulder use 11 rows. Ending in the Dark contrast. 11 rows should measure just over 10cm, (4in). CHECK that this is so. If not adjust the pattern accordingly at the next stage.
Continue in trebles and Main until 5(7,10,16,16)cm (2(3,4,5,6)in) have been worked.
Now introduce stripe pattern as follows:
Join in Light contrast and work 2 rows in treble. Fasten off.
Work 1 row in Main.
Join in Medium contrast and work 3 row treble. Fasten off Medium.
Work 1 row Main. Fasten off.
Join in Dark contrast and work 4 rows in treble. Fasten off.
Join in Main and work 5 rows in treble. **
Next row (back): 3ch, 105tr, (104sts)
Work 14cm (5½in) in total on these 104sts.
Add 115ch to end of this row at neck edge. (Depending upon where you finish your row this chain can be worked straight from the last stitch, or you will need to use a separate piece of yarn as for the body extensions earlier. If it is on a spare piece of yarn only 113 chain are required.)
Work on these 217 stitches until work measures exactly the number of rows from * to **.
Fasten off yarn and rejoin to 64th stitch.
Work on the central 91sts for second sleeve.
On these central stitches work the same number of straight rows that were needed to reach the underarm sleeve length, decreasing as follows:
Decrease 1st at each end of next two rows.
Work 1 row straight.
Decrease 1st at each end of the next 3 rows.
Work 1 row straight.
Rep the last 4 rows 3 times.

Work 14 rows treble.

Work 1 row dc. Fasten off.

Fold work as described at the beginning of the pattern and join underarm and sleeve seams all in one on the wrong side.

With 3.50mm hook work 3 rows dc. With RS facing work 1 row crab stitch. Fasten off.

Join Main colour in base of right front using 4.50mm hook.

Work 1 row dc using each stitch along front edges, dec 1 stitch at each side of the neck and work 3dc to 2 treble row ends across back neck, 1ch turn. Note: Watch that you have sufficient stitches, it is sometimes necessary to make an extra stitch on the first row at both beginning and end to keep base of garment flat.

Next row: 1ch, dc to end.

Next row: 1ch, dc to neck corner, dc2tog, dc across neck, dc2tog, dc to end. Rep last 2 rows until work is the required depth (approximately 15cm (6in) but this is entirely to taste). Complete with 1 row crab stitch using the 3.50mm hook and facing right side.

Belt

Make 10ch, using 3.50mm hook.

1dc in 3rd ch from hook, 1dc in each ch to end.

Row 2: 1ch dc to end.

Rep the last row until the length is sufficient for a tie-belt.

Note: Tie belts have a habit of stretching so err on the short rather than the long side.

PART THREE
Intermediate

JACOB'S JACKET

See opposite
Commercially produced yarn from a Jacob sheep's fleece, has all the off-white to deep brown/black patches combed together before spinning. This gives the wool an unusual natural look of brown grey. This commercial yarn was chosen for the main part of the button through jacket given below. A Suffolk fleece (also commercially spun) was selected to give lift and break the overall brown grey, incorporating the lighter wool in the bands at neck, hip and cuffs.

The design has an elegant tailored look suitable for town and country. It is an ideal 'match-maker' as the combing of the different patches of colour in the Jacob's fleece enables it to complement a wide range of shades. Horn buttons complete this picture of natural materials.

Materials: 600(700:750:850)g Forsell Special Breed Jacob's pure wool (M) 100(100:150:150)g contrast of Forsell's Suffolk pure wool (C). 6.00mm hook, buttons.
Note: If using large hooks and thicker yarn is new to you you may require an even larger hook.

Tension: 5sts and 4 rows in tr with 6.00mm hook to 6cm (2¼in)

Size: To fit bust 80(90,100,110)cm (32(35,39,42)in)
Back length: 60cm (23in)
Side Seam: 35cm (17in)
Depth of borders 5cm (2in)

TO MAKE
Body (fronts and back together)
In (M) make 111(123,129,141)ch.

Row 1: 1tr in 4th ch from hook, 1tr in each ch to end, 3ch, turn (109(121,127,139)sts).
Row 2: 1tr in each st to end, 3ch, turn.
Repeat row 2, 21 times.

First Front
Row 23: 27(30,31,34)tr, 3ch, turn (28(31,32,35)sts)
Work a further 14 rows in tr.
Row 38: 18(20,22,23)tr, 3ch, turn (19(21,23,24)sts)
Row 39: tr to end (no turning ch)
Work 2 rows as row 39.
Row 42: ss over 4(5,6,6)sts, 1ch, 4(5,5,5)dc, 5(5,6,6)htr, 5(5,5,6)tr.
Shoulder shaping now complete. Break off yarn.

Back
Rejoin yarn into next st of row 23, 3ch, 52(58,62,66)tr, 3ch, turn (53(59,63,69)sts).
Work 15 rows more of tr.
Break off yarn.

Second Front
Rejoin yarn into next st in row 23, tr to end, 3ch, turn. (28(32,32,35)sts).
Work a further 14 rows in tr.
Row 38: ss over 9(9,9,11)st, 3ch, tr to end, 3ch, turn (19(21,23,24)sts).
Row 39: to end, 3ch, turn.
Work 2 more rows in tr.
Row 42: 4(4,4,5)tr, 5(5,6,6)htr, 4(5,5,5)dc, 1ss.
Break off yarn.
Join shoulder seams by connecting the wedge shoulder edge to the corresponding stitches on the back.

Left Front Band
Row 1: With RS facing join (M) to top of left front, 1ch, dc to base putting 3dc to 2tr rows, with 1dc at corner, 1ch, turn.
Row 2: dc to end, 1ch, turn.
Row 3: As row 2. Break off yarn.
With safety pins or coloured thread mark the place for the buttons, place 1 marker 1st down from neck edge, and 1 marker 1st up from base (remember both neck and hip require bands). Place 3 more markers EVENLY spaced between the 2 markers already inserted.

Right Front Band
Row 1: With RS facing join in (M) to base of right front, 1ch, dc to end, 1ch, turn. Note: there must be the SAME number of stitches as in left front band.
Row 2: 1dc, *miss 1st, 1ch, dc to next marker, rep from * to end, 1ch, turn.
Row 3: As row 2 of left front. Break off yarn.

Sleeves (2 alike)

Make 33ch, in (M)

Row 1: 1tr in 4th ch from hook, 1tr in each ch to end, 3ch, turn (31sts).

Row 2: 1tr in same place as turning ch (1 inc made), tr to end, 3ch, turn.

Row 3: As row 2.

Row 4: tr to end (no inc), 3ch, turn.

Rep rows 2–4 inclusive 7 times (49sts).

Work row 2, 6 times (55sts). Adjust sleeve length if necessary. Break off yarn.

Cuff

Decide which is wrong side of work and have this facing. Join in C.

Row 1: *miss 2sts, 5tr in next st, miss 2sts, 1ss in next st, rep from * to end (6 shells). Leave loop in safety pin.

Row 2: With wrong side still facing join in (M) ** 3ch, 2tr in same st, ($\frac{1}{2}$ shell worked) *1ss in centre of 5tr, 5tr in ss, rep from * 3 times, 1ss in centre of 5tr, 2tr in lass ss, 1 more tr in this ss but catch loop in safety pin in with (M), work this tr until 2 loops remain, complete st with (C).

Row 3: *5tr in ss, 1ss in centre of shell, rep from * to end. Break off C.

Row 4: In (M) work as row 2 from **.

Row 5: Right side is now facing. Complete with 1 row crab st. Fasten off.

Join sleeve seams.

Attach sleeves to armhole.

Base Band

With wrong side facing join (C) to the right button band. Work first 5tr in first of the foundation chain (this makes the band width equal half a shell).

Continue as given for cuff (18(20,21,23)shells).

Neck

To a certain degree this band requires a little mathematical application.

Mark centre back neck st. This must be the centre of a shell.

Count 6sts and mark the centre of the next shells on either side.

At the front 5tr will be placed at the point where the button (hole) band joins the front. Count 6sts to the side of this and mark the centre of the next shell. Judge how many shells will be required between this marker and the one on the back. Slender necks need less than thicker necks.

Work the 5 rows as given for the cuff.

Sew buttons into place.

CIRCULAR TABLECLOTH

See opposite

Working in the round is not too difficult. In 'crochet lace', there are areas of solid work, plus areas of chain spaces. If the chains are not slack enough the open work will buckle the solid areas. In addition try to make the join look part of the pattern by watching how the ss lies at the end of every round. A little experimenting could help.

Materials: 21 balls Coats Chain Mercer–Crochet Cotton No. 20 (20g) 1.25mm hook.

Size: 163cm (65in) in diameter.

Tension: First 3 rows—6cm ($2\frac{3}{8}$in) in diameter.

TO MAKE

Commence with 15ch, join with ss to form a ring.

Row 1: 3 ch, 39tr into ring, 1ss into 3rd of 3ch.

Row 2: 3ch, leaving the last lp of each st on hook work 1 dtr into each of next 4tr, yoh draw through all lps on hook (4dtrcl made over 4sts), * 10ch, a 5 dtrcl over next 5tr, rep from * ending with 10ch, 1ss into 1st cl.

Row 3: * In next lp work 3dc (3ch, 4dc) twice 3ch and 3dc (3ps made), rep from * ending with 1ss into 1st dc.

Row 4: 1ss into each dc and into 1st p, 1dc into same p, * 3ch, into next p work 1tr 15ch and 1tr, (3ch, 1dc into next p) twice, rep from * omitting 1dc at end of last rep, 1ss into 1st dc.

Row 5: * 1dc into next lp, 29tr into next lp, 1dc into next lp, 3dc into next lp, rep from * ending with 1ss into 1st dc.

Row 6: 1ss into each of next 6tr, 5ch, * (miss 2tr, 1tr into next tr, 2ch) twice, miss 2tr, into next tr work 1tr 5ch and 1tr, (2ch, miss 2tr, 1tr into next tr) 3 times, 2ch, miss 5tr on next point, 1tr into next tr, 2ch, rep from * omit 1tr and 2ch at end of last rep, 1ss into 3rd of 5ch.

Row 7: * Into each of next 3 lps work 2dc p and 2dc, into next lp work 2dc p3 dc p and 2dc, into each of next 3lps work 2dc p and 2dc, 2dc into next lp; rep from * ending with 1ss into 1st dc. Fasten off.

Row 8: Miss 1st 3ps made on previous row, attach thread to next p, 1dc into same p, * 3ch, 1dc into next p, 9ch, miss next p, leaving the last lp of each on hook work 1tr into next p, miss next 2ps, 1 trip tr into next p, thread over and draw through all lps on hook (a joint trip tr made), 9ch, miss next p, 1dc into next p; rep from * omit 1dc at end of last rep, 1ss into 1st dc.

Row 9: 1dc into same place as ss, * 3dc into next lp, 1dc into next dc, 9dc into next lp, 1dc into sp between next joint trip tr, 9dc into next lp, 1dc into next dc; rep from * omit 1dc at end of last rep, 1ss into dc.

Row 10: 3ch, * 1tr into each dc within dc over joint trip tr, 3tr into next dc; rep from * ending with 1tr into each dc, 1ss into 3rd of 3ch.

Row 11: 1dc into next tr, * 3ch, miss 1tr, 1dc into next tr, (3ch, miss 2sts, 1dc into next tr) 8 times; rep from * omit 1dc at end of last rep, 1ss into 1st dc.

Row 12: 3dc into each lp, 1ss into 1st dc.

Row 13: 3ch, * 2tr into next dc, 1tr into each of next 26dc; rep from * omit 1tr at end of last rep, 1ss into 3rd of 3ch.

Row 14: As 2nd row missing 3tr between each cl and ending with 4ch, 1 quad tr into 1st cl.

Row 15: Into lp just made work 1dc a p 4dc p and 3dc; rep from * on 3rd row ending with into last lp work 3dc p and 3dc, 1ss into 1st dc.

Row 16: 1ss into next p, 1dc into same p, * 11ch, 1dc into centre p on next lp, rep from * ending with 5ch, 1 quad tr into first dc.

Row 17: As 15th row.

Row 18: As 16th row working 12ch lps instead of 11 and ending with 12ch, 1ss into 1st dc.

Row 19: As 3rd row working 4dc on each side of each p.

Row 20: As row working 19ch lps instead of 15ch lps.

Row 21: As 5th row working 37tr into lps instead of 29.

Row 22: 1ss into each of next 10tr, 5ch; rep from * on 6th row missing 9tr on each point instead of 5.

Row 23: As 7th row.

Row 24: As 8th row working 7ch lps instead of 9ch lps.

Row 25: As 9th row working 7dc instead of 9dc.

Row 26: As 10th row.

Row 27: * 1dc into next tr, 4ch, miss 3sts; rep from * ending with 1ss into 1st dc.

Row 28: 4dc into each lp, 1ss into 1st dc.

Row 29: 3ch, 1tr into each dc, 1ss into 3rd of 3ch.

Rep 27th–29th row once more.

Row 33–36: As 14th to 17th row.

Row 37: As 16th row working 12ch lps instead of 11 and ending with 6ch, 1 quad tr into 1st dc.

Row 38: As 15th row working 4dc on each side of each p.

Rep last 2 rows once more.

Row 41: As 18th row.

Row 42: As 19th row.

Row 43: As 4th row working 25ch lps instead of 15ch lps.

Row 44: As 5th row working 49tr into lps instead of 29.

Row 45: 1ss into next 16tr, 5ch, rep from * on 6th row missing 15tr instead of 5tr on each point and omit 2ch between each point.

Row 46: * 2dc into next lp, into each of next 2 lps work 2dc p and 2dc, into next lp work 2dc p 3dc p and 2dc, into each of next 2lps work 2dc p and 2dc, 2dc into next lp, rep from * ending with 1ss into 1st dc. Fasten off.

Row 47: Miss first 2ps made on previous row, attach thread to next p, 1dc into same p, * 3ch, 1dc into next p, 5ch, miss next p, a joint trip tr over next 2ps, 5ch, miss next p, 1dc into next p; rep from * omit 1dc at end of last rep, 1ss into 1st dc.

Row 48: As 9th row working 5dc instead of 9dc.
Row 49: 3ch, 1tr into each dc to within dc over 8th joint trip tr, 3tr into next dc, (1tr into each dc to within dc over next 7th joint trip tr, 3tr into next dc) 9 times, 1tr into each dc, 1ss into 3rd of 3ch.
Rep 27th to 29th row 3 times.
Row 59: 3ch, a 3dtr cl over next 3tr, * 10ch, miss 3tr, a 4dtr cl over next 4tr, 10ch, miss 3tr, a 5dtr cl over next 5tr; rep from * ending with 4ch, 1quad tr into 1st cl.
Rep 15th and 16th rows 4 times, then 15th row again.
Row 69: As 16th row working 12ch lps instead of 11 and ending with 6ch, 1quad tr into 1st dc.
Row 70: As 38th row.
Rep last 2 rows 4 times more.
Row 79: As 16th row working 13ch lps instead of 11 and ending with 6ch, 1 quin tr into first dc.
Row 80: As 15th row working 5dc instead of 3dc at beginning and end of each lp.
Rep last 2 rows 4 times more.

Edging
Row 1: 1ss into next p, 6ch, 1tr into same p, * 3ch, into next p work 1dc 3ch and 1dc (a p made over a p), 3ch (or 2ch less than number of dc made on last section of same ch on previous row—see note at beginning), working over previous row work 1dc into next dc on 2nd last row, 3ch (or same number as previous ch), a p over next p, 3ch, into next p work 1tr 3ch and 1tr, rep from * omitting 1tr 3ch and 1tr at end of last rep, 1ss into 3rd of 6ch.
Row 2: 1ss into next ch, 1ss into same sp, 16ch, 1tr into same sp, * 3ch, p over next p, 3ch (or same number as corresponding ch on previous row), ch), p over next p, 3ch, miss next tr into next sp work 1tr 13ch and 1tr; rep from * omit 1tr 13ch and 1tr at end of last rep, 1ss into 3rd of 16ch.
Row 3: 1ss into 1st lp, 4ch, * 22dtr into same lp, p over next p, 2ch (or 1ch less than number of ch on previous row), p over next p, miss next tr, 1dtr into next lp; rep from * omit 1dtr at end of last rep, 1ss into 4th of 4ch. Fasten off.

Damp and press.

CANDY FLOSS BLOUSE

See page 46.
A cool and comfortable blouse for warm summer evenings. Using the ribbon yarn for the contrast bands needs careful control and a smaller hook. This is one of those patterns where it is prudent to count the sts when using the ribbon yarn, and for the first row of the Pearl cotton.

Materials: 2 balls Pearl (yarn B): 2 balls Pearl (yarn C): 2 balls Pearl (yarn D): 2 balls Cabaret (yarn A) for bands: 4.50mm and 5.00mm hooks.

Size: To fit bust 82(92,112)cm (32(36,40)in)

Tension: Worked in Pearl with size 5.00mm over 'V'-stitch, pattern 10sts over 7.5cm (3in)

TO MAKE:

Back

With yarn A and 4.50mm hook make 67(73,79)ch.
Row 1: 1htr in 4th ch from hook, htr to end. (65(71,77)sts)
No turning ch.
Row 2: (WS is now facing), *1tr, 1ss, rep from * to end, 2ch, turn.
Row 3: htr to end. Fasten off.
Row 4: At the BEGINNING of row 3 join in yarn B to the turning ch using 5.00mm hook. 3ch, miss 2sts (because the work has not been turned it will look as though only 1st has been missed) *2tr in next st, miss 1st, rep from * to last 2sts, 1st in last st (68(74,80)sts).
Row 5: 3ch, turn, *2tr in centre of 2tr of row below (insert hook in space) rep from * to last st, 1tr in last st.
Rep row 5, 7 times. Fasten off.
Row 13: Rejoin yarn A to beginning of row 12 using 4.50mm hook, 2ch, 1htr in same place as turning ch, 1htr in each st to last st, 2htr in last st (70(76, 82)sts).
Row 14: no turning ch, 1tr in same place as yarn emerges, * 1ss, 1tr, rep from * to last st, 1ss in last st (71(77,83)sts)
Row 15: htr to end. Fasten off.
Row 16: Join in yarn C with 5.00mm hook, work as row 4.
Rep row 5, 14 times. Fasten off.
Work rows 13–15 once.
With 5.00mm hook and yarn D work as row 4.
Rep row 5, 20 times.
Next row: With 4.50mm hook and yarn A join to beginning of last row. 2ch, 1htr in same place 1htr, *2htr in next st, 5htr rep from * to last 4sts, 3htr, 2htr in last st.
Next row as row 14 ●
Prepare Next Row: Use 2 safety pins to mark central 40sts. After next row has been worked, each st either side of the pin should have a 6ch loop, one 6ch loop should be at edge of shoulder seam. Place markers to show where to position 2 further 6 chain loops on each shoulder between the neck and the arm.
Work this row: 2ch, * htr to marker, 6ch rep from * to end. Fasten off.

Front

Work as back to ●
Final row: Place front to back and mark on the front where the 6ch loops of back lie. 2ch, 1htr, *ss to centre of matching 6ch loop of

back, htr to next marker, rep from * to end.
Join side seams (up to and including 3 bands of yarn A)

Armholes
With RS facing commence at shoulders using 4.50mm hook and yarn D. Omit the neck band in yarn A and put 1dc in each row to side seam join. Continue with 1dc in each row end up the other piece, finishing just before the band at neck in yarn A.

CROSSED CABLE SWEATER

See page 50

Aran-style crochet can be created in two ways—(a) surface crochet (b) incorporating texture with stitches in the pattern as the work progresses.

The crossed raised trebles in this pattern are used to simulate the cable stitch of knitting but often this creates a gap in the crochet if not carefully controlled. It is this need for care where the raised trebles cross that causes a fairly large number of Aran-style patterns to use the surface crochet method.

Materials: 10(11,13) 50g balls of pure aran Wendy: 5.00mm and 5.50mm crochet hooks.

Size: To fit bust/chest 92(102,112)cm (36(40,44)in)

Actual size: 99(109,119)cm (39(43,47)in)

Tension: 5tr to 7cm worked on trebles.

Additional abbreviations:
RdtrFL—Raised double treble at front leaning to the left with RS facing
RdtrFR—Raised double treble at front leaning to the right with RS facing
RdtrBL—Raised double treble at back leaning to the left with RS facing
RdtrBR—Raised double treble at back leaning to the right with RS facing
One popcorn equals 6tr in next st, remove hook insert hook into 1st tr and pull loop through

TO MAKE:

Back

With 5.50mm hook make 62(68,74)ch.

Row 1: 1tr in 4th ch from hook, tr to end, 3ch, turn, (60(66,72)sts)

Row 2: 0(3,6)tr, 2RtrF * 1tr, 1RdtrFL, 2tr, 1 popcorn, 2tr, 1RdtrFR, 1ch, 1RdtrFL round next tr, miss 1st, 2tr, 1 popcorn, 2tr, 1RdtrFR, 1tr ** 3RtrF, rep from * once, rep from * to ** once, 2RtrF, 1(4,7)tr, 3ch, turn.

Row 3: 0(3,6)tr, 2RtrB, *2tr, 1RdtrBR (Note: Do not work into next stitch top as raised double treble is that stitch), 2tr, 1RdtrBL, 3tr, 1RdtrBR, 3tr, 1RdtrBL, 2tr, 3RtrB, ** rep from * once, rep from * to ** once, 2RtrB, 1(4,7)tr, 3ch, turn (64(70,76)sts).

Row 4: 0(3,6)tr, 2RtrF*, 3tr, 1RdtrFL, 1tr, 1RdtrF, 5tr, 1RdtrFL, 1tr, 1RdtrFR, 3tr, ** 3RtrF, rep from * once and from * to ** once, 2RtrF, 1(4,7)tr, 3ch, turn.

Row 5: 0(3,6)tr, 2RtrB* 3tr, 1RdtrBR, 1ch, 1RdtrBL, (to form a cross-over of the Rdtr at the point of the diamond), 2tr, 1 popcorn, 2tr, 1RdtrBR, 1ch, 1RdtrBL, 3tr, ** 3RtrB, rep from * once and from * to ** once, 2RtrB, 1(4,7)tr, 3ch, turn.

Row 6: 0(3,6)tr, 2RtrF, *2tr, 1RdtrFR, 3tr, 1RdtrFL, 3tr, 1RdtrFR, 3tr, 1RdtrFL, 2tr, ** 3RtrF, rep from * once and from * to ** once, 2RtrF, 1(4,7)tr, 3ch, turn.

Row 7: 0(3,6)tr, 2RtrB, *1tr, 1RdtrBL, 5tr, 1RdtrBR, 1tr, 1RdtrBL, 5tr, 1RdtrBR, 1tr, ** 3RtrB, rep from * once and from * to ** once, 2RtrB, 1(4,7)tr, 3ch, turn.

Row 8: 0(3,6)tr, 2RtrF* 1tr, 1RdtrF, 2tr, 1 popcorn, 2tr, 1RdtrFL, 1ch, 1RdtrFR, 2tr, 1 popcorn, 2tr, 1RdtrF, 1tr** 3RtrF, rep from * once and from * to ** once, 2RtrB, 1(4,7)tr, 3ch, turn.

Rows 3–8 inclusive form the pattern.

Rep pattern 5 times (7 for a longer length)●.

Rep row 3–4 inclusive once.

Fasten off.

Welt

Rejoin yarn to foundation ch and with 5.00mm hook work 7cm (2½in)

Raised treble rib (see page 95)

Front

Work as back to ●

Place 2 safety pins to mark central 20sts (central panel).

Work 1½ patterns (8 rows) on EACH of the remaining 21(24,27)sts for the shoulders.

Fasten off.

Work welt as for back.

Sleeves

With 5.50mm hook make 34ch.

Row 1: 1tr in 4th ch from hook, tr to end, (32sts).

Row 2: 1tr in same place as turning ch, (for an increase), 5tr, 2RtrF, work from * to ** once of row 2 of back, 2RtrF, 5tr, 2tr in last st, 3ch, turn.

Continue keeping pattern up centre of sleeves by working 2 Raised trebles before and after the asterisks and working between the asterisk of pattern rows once.

Increase 1st into each end of every 3rd row until work measures 40cm (16½in).

Fasten off.

Cuff

Rejoin yarn to foundation chain using 5.00mm hook and work 5–8cm (2–3in) raised treble rib or until sleeve is the correct length.

Join sleeve to body, carefully centralising the panel of the sleeve to match the shoulder.

Join sleeve and side seam in one.

Neck

Using the 5.00mm hook work raised treble rib round neck for as deep as required. If desired it can be extended for a polo neck.

Fasten off.

PRINCESS DIANA COLLAR

See page 51

Princess Diana re-introduced the detachable collar to the fashion scene and it has retained great popularity. The design given here has sufficient depth to be used as a detachable collar, alternatively, omit the last row of the pattern and insert into a fabric blouse or dress as a yoke. The last two rows of the design can be used as an edging to sleeves, hems, pockets, etc. (That is Row 16, *5ch, miss 2sts, 1dc in next st, rep from * to end. Then work Row 17 into these loops.)

Materials: 2 balls 20's cotton DMC: 1.25mm crochet hook for small neck: 1.50mm crochet hook medium neck: 1.75mm crochet hook for large neck: sufficient narrow ribbon to thread through collar which can be secured at each end or made longer to use as a tie.

TO MAKE:
Make 123ch.
Row 1: 1tr in 4th ch from hook, 1tr in each ch to end (121sts)
Row 2: 5ch, 1quad tr *5ch, miss 5sts, 2quad trs, rep from * to end 3ch, turn.
Row 3: tr to end, 4ch, turn.

Row 4: miss 2sts, 1dc in next st, *3ch, miss 2sts, 1dc, rep from * to end, 4ch, turn.
Row 5: 1dc in sp *3ch 1dc 3ch 1dc in next sp, 3ch, 1dc in next st, rep from * to last sp, 3ch 1dc 3ch 1dc in last sp.
Row 6: As row 5.
The neck stand is complete but do not break off yarn. Continue down the edge with 3ch 1dc to make the edge similar to that of the last row of the neck stand.

Main Collar Part

Working into the foundation chain again:
Row 1: 5ch, 1dc in 6th st, *5ch, miss 4sts, 1dc in next st, rep from * to end.
Row 2: *5ch, 1dc in sp, 2ch, 3tr cl in dc, 2ch, 1dc in sp, rep from * to last sp, 5ch, 1dc in centre of ch of last sp (into the actual stitch).
Row 3: 5ch, 1dc in sp, *1ch, 3dtr cl in cl, 4ch, 1ss in cl, 4ch, 3dtr cl in cl, 1ch, 1dc in sp, 5ch, 1dc in same sp, rep from * to end (with the last dc being worked in centre st of sp)
Row 4: *5ch, 1dc in sp, 5ch, 1dc in cl, 2ch, 3dtr cl in ss, 2ch, 1dc in cl, rep from * to last sp, 5ch, 1dc in sp, 3ch, 1tr in same sp.
Row 5: 5ch, 1dc in sp, *5ch, 1dc in cl, 5ch, 1dc in sp, 5ch, 1dc in same sp, rep from * to end, 3ch, 1tr in last sp.
Row 6: *5ch, 1dc in sp, rep from * to end, 2ch, 1tr in last sp.
Row 7: *2ch, 1 3tr cl in dc, 2ch, 1dc in sp, 5ch, 1dc in next sp, 5ch, 1dc in same sp, 5ch, 1dc in next sp, rep from * to last sp, 2ch, 3tr cl in dc, 2ch, 1dc in last sp, 2ch, 1tr in end, 1ch, turn.
Row 8: *1ch, 3dtr cl in cl, 4ch, 1ss in cl, 4ch, 3dtr cl in cl, 1ch, 1dc in sp, (5ch, 1dc in next sp) twice, rep from * to last cl, 1ch, 3dtr cl in cl, 4ch, 1ss in cl, 4ch, 3dtr cl in cl, 1ch, 1dc in end.
Row 9: *2ch, 3tr cl in ss, 2ch, 1dc in next cl, (5ch, 1dc) twice, 1dc in cl, rep from * to last ss, 2ch, 3tr cl in ss, 2ch, 1dc in cl.
Row 10: 7ch, 1dc in cl, *(5ch, 1dc in sp) twice, 5ch, 1dc in same sp, 5ch, 1dc in same sp, 5ch, 1dc in cl, rep from * to end, 4ch, 1dtr in end.
Row 11: *5ch, 1dc in next sp, rep from * to last sp, 3ch, 1dtr.
Row 12: (5ch, 1dc in next sp) 3 times, *1ch, 3tr cl in next dc, 1ch, 1dc in sp, (5ch, 1dc in next sp) 4 times, rep from * to last 3sps, 1ch, 3tr cl in next dc, 1ch, 1ch, 1dc in sp, (5ch, 1dc in next sp) twice, 3ch, 1dtr in end.
Row 13: (5ch, 1dc in next sp) twice *1ch, 3dtr cl in cl, 4ch, 1ss in same place, 4ch, 3dtr cl, 1ch, 1dc in next sp (5ch, 1dc in next sp) 3 times, rep from * to last cl, 1ch, 3dtr cl in cl, 4ch, 1ss in same place, 3ch, 3dtr cl, 1ch, 1dc in next sp, (5ch, 1dc) twice, 3ch, 1dtr in end.
Row 14: (5ch, 1dc in next sp) twice, 5ch, 1dc in cl, *2ch, 3dtr cl in ss, 2ch, 1dc in ch, (5ch, 1dc in next sp) 4 times, rep from * to last 2sps (5ch, 1dc in sp) twice, 3ch, 1dtr in last st.
Row 15: 5ch, 1dc in sp (5ch, 1dc in next sp, 5ch, 1dc in same sp) twice, *(5ch, 1dc in 2ch sp) twice, (5ch, 1dc in next sp, 5ch, 1dc in same sp) 6 times, rep from * to last 3sps, (5ch, 1dc in next sp, 5ch, 1dc in same sp) twice, 5ch, 1dc in last sp.
Row 16: *5ch, 1dc in next sp, 5ch, 1dc in same sp, 5ch, 1dc in next sp, rep from * to end, 5ch, 1dc in last st.

Side Edge

Without breaking the yarn, work up this side of the collar in dc keeping a straight edge, 1ch, turn and work 1dc in each stitch down to the end of the collar.

Row 17: *4ch, 1dc in next sp, 4ch, 1dc in same place, 4ch, 1dc in next sp, rep from * to end.

Last Side Edge

Either work in dc as the other side or continue in tiny loops as at the neck. Fasten off.

Use press studs for a neat fastener, alternatively have extra ribbon length to be used as a tie.

CHEVRON BATWING

See cover photograph

This exotic sweater in mohair and slub contrast is based on chevrons, giving it an attractive fan shape. Different, rich looking and luxurious, the jersey is not as difficult to execute as it looks.

Materials: 6 balls Sirdar Nocturne(M): 4 balls Sirdar Mosaic (C): 6.00mm hook.

Size: Due to its drawstring waist and fan shape, this is one size to fit up to 105cm (41in) bust and 85cm (33in) waist.

Tension: 5trs worked on 6.00mm hook to 5cm (2in) approximately. (The mohair was held looser than when crocheting with smooth yarns. If this is not done use 7.00mm hook holding the hook well away from the hook head.)

TO MAKE

Make 57ch in C.

Row 1: 1tr in 4th ch from hook, 1tr in each ch to end (55sts)

Row 2: (Shaping row) In C 4ch, *1tr, 1htr, 1dc, 1htr, 1tr, 1dtr, Repeat from * to end. Break off yarn.

Row 3: In M 3ch, 1tr in same place, *1tr, 3trcl (over 3sts), 1tr, 3tr in dtr. Repeat from * to end. (Only 2tr in last st)

Row 4: 3ch, 1tr in same place, *1tr, 3trcl over 3sts, 1tr, 3tr in next st, rep from * to end (only 2tr in last st)

Row 5: In M (inc row) 3ch, 2tr in same place as turning chain *1tr, 3trcl, 1tr, 5tr in next st, rep from * to end (only 3tr in last st) Leave loop in safety pin.

Row 6: In C 3ch, 1tr in same place, *2tr, 3trcl, 2tr, 3tr in next st, rep from * to end (only 2tr in last stitch) Fasten off yarn.

Row 7: In M do not turn work bring up the yarn from row 5 3ch and work as row 6.

Row 8: As row 7.

Row 9: (Inc row) 3ch, 2tr in same place as turning ch, *2tr, 3trcl, 2tr, 5tr in next st, rep from * to end (only 3tr in end st) DO NOT TURN WORK.

Row 10: Join C to beginning of last row 3ch, 1tr in same place as turning ch, *3tr, 3trcl, 3tr, 3tr in next st, rep from * to end (only 2tr in last st).

Row 11: In M work as row 10.

Row 12: As row 11.

Row 13: Work an increase row by placing 2 extra trs in the points.

Row 14: In C keep pattern continuous by working 4trs between increases and decreases.

Rows 15 and 16 as row 14 in M.

Row 17: (Inc row) In M.

The sides up to this point will be in the seam of the sweater. You may wish now to cut off the yarns when changing colour to prevent a colour drag showing. There is a cuff however so it is not entirely necessary.

Row 18: In C with 5trs between increases and decreases.

Row 19, 20 and 21 as row 18 but in M.

Row 22: In C as row 18.

Rows 23–25 as rows 19–21.

Row 26: In C join to first st *1dc, 1htr, 2tr, 2dtr, 1trtr, 2dtr, 2tr, 1htr, 1dc, 1ss rep from * twice ** 1ss, 1dc, 1htr, 3tr, 3trcl (5tr, 3tr in next st, 5tr, 3trcl) twice, 3tr, 1htr, 1dc, 1ss, rep from * to ** 3 times. Fasten off.

Return to base and join in C to foundation ch.

Work row 2 of M once break off yarn.

Next row: In M work row 3 once.

Next row: Work row 5 once and fasten off.

Work another piece to match.

Side Seams

Leaving the top 12 rows (excluding levelling row) join the rest for the two side seams.

Join shoulders across row 26 where the chevron has been levelled out, using C yarn.

Cuff

In C work 1dc in each row end, 1dc at underarm, and 3dc at shoulder (28sts), 1ch, turn.

Next row: 1 row dc to end ss to join and fasten off.

Work other cuff to match.

Tie

Using 3 thicknesses of C yarn tog make a crochet chain sufficiently long to thread through the first row of trebles and to tie at front.

PART FOUR

More Difficult

CHANTELEINE

See page 58

The use of the second contrast yarn (which is thick and braid like) gives the appearance of a ribbon threaded through. Not only is this a satisfying pattern to work but the sweater can be worn for day or evening; with skirt or trousers: as a sweater or an overtop—a sufficiently versatile garment for anyone.

Materials: 300g Tiana Chanteleine in Main (M): 50g Tiana Chanteleine in Contrast (C): 50g Mylene Chanteleine Braid Yarn (B): 8.00mm Crochet Hook.

Size: Medium

Tension: 5sts to 5cm (2in): 4 rows to 9cm (3½in)

TO MAKE:

(2 Alike)
This garment is worked from the neck down to the waist so the strip should measure 117cm (46in).
Using the 8.00mm crochet hook make 117ch in M.
Row 1: 1tr in 4th ch from hook, 1tr in each ch to end (115sts)
Do not break off this yarn.
Row 2: Join in (B) to the first stitch of row 1 (that is the turning chain before the 1st treble), 2ch, miss 1st, 1dc in next st, *1ch, miss 1st, 1dc in next st, rep from * to end. Break off yarn. Turn work.
Row 3: Insert hook into the last dc made in (B) and draw through (M), 3ch, *1tr under ch of (B) into the tr of Row 1, loop the thread up to avoid a pucker, 1tr in dc, rep from * to end. Do not turn work but join in (A) to the beginning of Row 2.
Row 4: *1dtr, 1dc, rep from * to end, turn work.
Row 5: Insert hook into the dc just made and draw (M) through, 3ch, 1tr in each st to end. Do not turn work.

Rep rows 2–5 twice.

Row 14: ss over 14sts, 1dc, 1htr, 83tr, 1htr, 1dc, 1ss (leaving 13sts unworked) (89sts) Continue only in (M), turning work on each row as in other patterns.

Row 15: ss over 8, 1dc, 1htr, 68tr, 1htr, 1dc, 1ss (72sts).

Row 16: ss over 5, 1dc, 1htr, 68tr, 1htr, 1dc, 1ss.

Repeat row 16 twice (42sts).

Work 12 rows in treble on these 42sts. Break off yarn.

Work another piece exactly the same.

One side of the yoke looks different from the other.

The more textured side is the right side. With wrong sides together join the tops of the sleeves and shoulders by double crocheting the two pieces together for 44sts on each side leaving 27sts unworked for the neck opening. Join underarm and sleeve seams in one.

You may find that a *loose* oversewing stitch will be best for this.

Neck

With RS facing in (M) work 1 row dc, join with ss.

Still with RS facing work 1 row Crab stitch round the neck opening.

Cuff and Hip

In (M) and RS facing work 1 row dc, join with ss.

Still with RS facing crab stitch round sleeve edges and base edge.

Tie: make a length of chain using 1 strand B and 2 strands of A together and thread this fairly soft but thicker chain through the last row of trebles worked to form a drawstring.

CHARLESTON

See page 59

The ribbon yarn used in this design is slippy and must be secured firmly if the whole is not to unravel like some nightmare or cartoon. The silky feel and the sheen of the ribbon contrasts yet complements the matt finish of the thicker heavily textured yarn. The contrast between a vibrant single colour to a muted mixture, completes the blending of contrasts into the overtop design.

Changes can be made by lengthening the sleeves and/or removing the fringe.

Note: A sewing needle and thread, the same colour as the ribbon yarn used, is a useful safety measure after ends have been threaded through, to prevent them working loose.

The garment is worked from the centre back and the centre front sideways to the ends of the sleeves.

Materials: Main (M) 10(12,14) 50g balls Avocet Garbo: Contrast (C) 2(2,3) balls Avocet Soiree. Note: A third Soiree is needed for the first two sizes if fringing is included: 5.00mm and 7.00mm hooks.

Size: To fit bust 86(96,102)cm (34(38,40)ins)

Tension: 9sts to 10cm (4in) worked in trs with the Garbo yarn and 7.00mm hook

TO MAKE
Left Back
Make 53ch with the Garbo yarn (M). As this chain is worked into again for the other side you can make them VERY loose. That is, a little bigger than the exact circumference of the main stem part of the hook.
Row 1: Work 1tr in 4th ch from hook, (do not count loop on hook), 1tr in each ch to end. Do not break off this yarn (51sts).
Row 2: Join in Soiree yarn (C) 1ch, turn, 1dc 1ch in each backloop of st to end. Fasten off yarn. DO NOT TURN work.
Row 3: Lift (M) up side of last row with a ss, 3ch (this is your first st), 1tr in front loop of each of remaining 50sts, 3ch, turn.
Row 4: 1tr in each st to end, leave loop in safety pin.

Left Front
Make 33ch.
Row 1: 1tr in 4th ch from hook, 28tr, 2tr 1dtr 1ch in last st (33sts).
Row 2: Join in (C), 2ch, 1dc 1ch in back loop of each st to end. Fasten off.
Row 3: Lift (M) up side of last row 1ch through 2ch of (C) 5ch 1dtr 2tr in same place, tr in each front loop to end (37sts).
Row 4: 3ch, 35tr, 2tr, 1dtr in turning ch of row 3, 14ch, attach this chain to top of turning ch in corresponding row of back. Fasten off.

Left Back and Front
Row 5: Rejoin (C) to back using loop in safety pin.
Work 1dc 1ch in back loop of each st (including each ch) to end. (104sts).
Row 6: As row 3.
Row 7: tr to end.
Row 8: As row 2.
Rep rows 6–8 inclusive 3(4,5) times.
Then rows 6 and 7 once.
Break off yarns.
On central 43sts work 1 row tr in M.
Work rows 7, 8 and 6, 3 times and then rows 7 and 8 once.
Fasten off.

Right Back and Front
Work exactly as Left Front but place the ribbon yarn in the *FRONT* loop of each st and the Garbo yarn in the *BACK* loop of each st. Join centre fronts.

Join centre backs.
Join underarms and side seams as one.
Leave the ribbon ends on the right side and incorporate into an underarm fringe.

Base Fringe
Cut as many 60cm (24in) lengths of ribbon as you wish (that is a 30cm (12in) finished length) of fringe. These require looping into the base line at intervals.
Note: It may be necessary to use sewing thread and needle to stitch the ribbon into place.

Neck
With a 5.50mm hook, commence at centre back neck with ribbon yarn to work 1 row dc round neck. Decrease 1st at each side of back neck, and 2sts in the centre front point. Join with a ss.
Final row: Crab st to end.
Fasten off securely.

MOTIF BEDSPREAD

See page 62
The two shades of pink (or whatever colour you choose) gives this bedspread a distinctive look. A little more care is required when working the design as it uses a filler between motifs and has a raised floral effect.

Materials: 46 balls Pale Pink (A) and 23 balls Shaded Pink (B) of Coats Chain Mercer–Crochet No. 20 (20g). 1.25mm hook.

Size: Motif—15cm (6in) measured over 2 coils and centre rose. Finished size 180 × 240cm (71 × 95in)

TENSION: First coil 5.5 × 6cm($2\frac{1}{8}$ × $2\frac{3}{8}$in)

TO MAKE

First Coil
Row 1: Using A 16ch, 1ss into 1st ch—1st circle made, 39ch, 1ss into 16th ch from hook—2nd circle made, 1ch, turn.
Row 2: 1dc into each of next 15ch, 1dc into same ch as ss, 1dc into each of next 23ch 1dc into same ch as next ss, 1dc into each of next 15ch, 1ss into same ch as next ss on previous row, 3ch, turn.
Row 3: Miss 1st ss, 1tr into next dc, (2ch, 1tr into next dc) 9 times, *(1ch, miss 1dc, 1tr into next dc) twice, 1ch, miss 1dc, into next dc work 1tr 3ch and 1tr—a corner sp made, 1ch, miss 1dc, 1tr into next dc, rep from * 3 times, (1ch, miss 1dc, 1tr into next dc) twice,

(2ch, 1tr into next dc) 9 times, 3ch, 1ss into same place as next ss on 1st row, turn.

Row 4: Into 1st 3ch sp work 1dc 1htr and 1tr, 3tr into each of next 9sps, *2t into each of next 3sps, 5tr into next corner sp, 2tr into next sp, rep from * 3 times, 2tr into each of next 2sps, 3tr into each of 7sps, miss 1st 6tr made on opposite circle, remove lp from hook, insert hook into next tr and draw dropped lp through, 1tr into next sp—a joining tr made, (a joining tr into same sp) twice, 3tr into next sp, into last sp work 1tr 1htr and 1dc, 1ss into same place as next ss on 1st row. Fasten off.

Second Coil

Work as 1st coil until 7 groups of 3tr have been completed on 4th row, 1tr into next sp, miss 16 free tr to left of joining on first coil, join next tr by working a joining tr into same sp on second coil, 1tr into same sp, complete as first coil.

Make 2 more coils joining each as 2nd coil was joined to first and joining last coil to 1st coil to correspond.

Centre Rose

Using B commence with 8ch, join with ss to form a ring.

Row 1: 7ch, into ring work (1tr, 4ch) 7 times, 1ss into 3rd of 7ch.

Row 2: Into each sp work 1dc 1htr 3tr 1htr and 1dc, 1ss into back lp of 1st dc.

Row 3: Working from the back work 1dc into back lp of 3rd of 7ch on 1st row, (4ch, 1dc into back lp of next tr on 1st row) 7 times, 4ch, 1ss into 1st dc.

Row 4: Into each lp work 1dc 1htr 4tr 1htr and 1dc, 1ss into back lp of 1st dc.

Row 5: Working from the back work 1dc into back lp of 1st dc on 2nd last row, (5ch, 1dc into back lp of next dc on same row) 7 times, 5ch, 1ss into 1st dc.

Row 6: As 4th row working 5tr instead of 4.

Row 7: As 5th row working 6ch instead of 5.

Row 8: Into next lp work 1dc 1htr and 3tr, miss 8 free tr to left of joining between any 2 coils, join next tr by working a joining tr into same lp on rose, into same lp work 3tr 1htr and 1dc—a joining petal made, * a joining petal joining to 8th free tr on opposite side of coil, a joining petal joining to 9th free tr to left of next joining between coils; rep from * 3 times omitting a joining petal at end of last rep, 1ss into 1st dc. Fasten off.

Second Motif

First coil: work as first coil to within 2nd corner on 4th row, into next corner sp work 2tr and a joining tr joining to corresponding tr on first motif, 2 joining tr into same sp, 2 joining tr into each of next 4sps, into next corner sp work 3 joining tr and 2tr, complete as first motif.

Make 12 rows of 16 motifs, joining adjacent coils as second motif was joined to first leaving one corner free on each coil between joinings.

Filling

Work as centre rose for 5 rows.

Row 6: 1ss into next ch and into lp, * into same work 1htr 7tr and 1htr, insert hook into same lp and draw thread through, insert hook into next lp and draw thread through, thread over and draw through all lps on hook—a joint dc made, rep from * working last joint dc into last lp and 1st lp, 1ss into 1st htr. Fasten off.

Row 7: Attach A to centre tr on any petal, 7ch, 2dtr into same place as join, * 4ch, 1dc into next joint dc, 4ch, into centre tr on next petal work 2dtr 3ch and 2dtr; rep from * omitting 2dtr 3ch and 2dtr at end of last rep, 1dtr into same place as join, 1ss into 4th 7ch.

Row 8: 1ss into next lp, 4ch, 1dtr into same lp, 4ch, 1ss into centre tr on any corner between joinings, 4ch—a joining lp made, * 2dtr into same lp on filling, 6ch 1dc into next dc, 6ch, 2dtr into next 3ch lp, a joining lp into centre tr on next corner between joinings; rep from * omit 2dtr and a joining lp at end of last rep, 1ss into 4th of 4ch. Fasten off.

Fill in all spaces between motifs in this manner.

Damp and pin out to measurements.

SERENADE

See page 66

The use of three colours over a two pattern design staggers the striped effect of the colours to give an asymmetrical look. This pattern uses crab stitch for a textured ridge effect either side of the narrow stripes. Connecting these two ridges during working gives the illusion of the stripe sinking behind the actual garment. The only difficult part of this pattern is in catching the crab stitch down and making sure that the new colour does not lose any stitches as this is worked behind the crab stitch, using the same stitches that the crab stitch has already used.

Although it would be difficult to find better yarns than the Sirdar for this pattern, it can be succesfully worked in a cotton range for the summer months.

Materials: 200g Sirdar Secrets DK in Chocolate Bronze: (A) 200g Sirdar Wash'n'Wear Desert Sand (C) 200g Sirdar Casino Golden Nougat: (B) Hook size: 6.00mm

Size: One-size (depending on number of stitches placed in the waist this can fit up to a 107cm (42in))

Tension: 6sts to 5cm (2in) worked in trebles in Wash'n'Wear yarn

TO MAKE
Work from cuff to cuff.
With A make 27ch.
Row 1: 1tr in 4th ch from hook, 1tr in each ch to end, 1ch, turn.
Row 2: 1dc in same place as turning ch, dc to last st, 2dc in last st, 3ch, turn. (2incs made)
Row 3: tr to end, 1ch, turn.
Row 4: As row 2 (29sts).
Row 5: RS is now facing, 1ch, 1 crab st, *catch next crab st round tr of row below, 5 crab st, rep from * to last 3sts, catch next crab st round tr, 2 crab st, fasten off.
Row 6: Join B with RS facing to start of row 4 [that is behind the crab st] 3ch, 1tr in each st in row 4 (29sts)
Row 7: 3ch, inc 1tr, tr to last 2sts, 2tr in last st, break off B.
Row 8: Join in C, 1ch, dc to end.
Row 9: 1ch, *5 crab st, catch next crab st to crab st of row 5, rep from * to last 5sts, 5 crab st.
Row 10: As row 2.
Row 11: 3ch, 3tr, *catch next tr into crab st of row 9, 5tr rep from * to last 5sts, catch next tr into crab st of row 9, 4tr, 1ch, turn.

Row 12: As row 2.
Row 13: As row 3.
Rep row 2 and 3 once and row 2 once more, (39sts)
Rows 2 and 3 form the stitch pattern of wider stripes.
Rows 5–11 inclusive form the relief ribbon-look pattern.
Check that all catch stitches sit over the catch stitches of the previous ribbon-look section.
Row 17: 1ch, *5crab st, catch down as on row 5, rep from * to last 6sts, crab st to end.
Row 18: In A, as row 6.
Row 19: In A, as row 7, fasten off.
Row 20: In B, as row 8.
Row 21: 1ch, 4crab st *catch down next st as on row 9, 5crab st, rep from * to end.
Row 22: As row 10.
Row 23: As row 11 catching centre st of the 5.
Rep rows 2 and 3, 3 times.
Row 30: As row 2.
Row 31: As row 5 ensuring catch sts are in line with previous ribbon-look stripe.
Row 32: In C, as row 6.
Row 33: In C, as row 7.
In A Work rows 8–11 inclusive keeping catch sts in line.
Rep rows 2 and 3, 5 times (71sts).
Work row 2 once.
Row 49: tr to end, make 15ch.
Using a spare piece of yarn A, work 14ch and attach to the starting ch of row 49 just worked. Fasten off the spare yarn and return to the first length of ch.
Row 50: 1dc in 3rd ch from hook, 1dc in rem 12ch, dc across row 49, continue in dc across ch (101sts).
Row 51: Crab st throughout catching down every 6th st to keep line of pattern.
Row 52 and 53 in tr using B yarn.
Row 54: In C work rows 8–11 inclusive without increasing and keeping catch sts in line.
Work 1 row dc.
Work 1 row tr.
Rep these 2 rows 5 times.
Work row 5 once (101sts).
Next row: In yarn A work as row 6 until 51sts have been made, 3ch, turn.
Next row: As row 7.
Work rows 8–11 inclusive.

Divide for Neck Split
Using Yarn C and 49sts.
Work 1 row dc
Work 1 row tr
Rep these 2 rows 6 times, leave yarn attached (one side of the neck completed).
Miss 3sts and rejoin yarn C to next st.

Work (1 row dc, 1 row tr) 7 times on the remaining 49sts.
Fasten off this yarn.
Return to other yarn C still attached.

Second side and sleeve
Work to match first side.
Note: If the decreases are worked on the tr row, they will be at exactly the same place as the increase which was worked on the dc row.
Join underarm and side seams.

Neck
Join yarn C to centre back neck dc to split, dc3tog (to gather in and round off neck slit) dc across front, dc3tog at side, dc to centre back, join with ss. Fasten off.

Welt
In yarn A work sufficient trs to fit where the sweater is to be worn ie hip or waist.
On 4.50mm hook work 1 row trs round front and back of sweater.
60trs were used for a 72cm (28in) waist.
Work 4 rows raised treble rib.
Change to 4.00mm hook.
Continue in raised treble rib until required depth of welt is reached.
Fasten off.

Cuffs
For shorter arms the first band of colour can be turned back and narrow elastic inserted.
For larger arms work a raised treble rib as given for the welt.

AFGHAN WAISTCOAT

See page 70
A long line waistcoat with a difference. Working loop stitch is not the easiest technique to master as it is important to have all loops the same size. In addition it is quite easy to have too many stitches in the border when working the first row, because of the density of the texture of the yarn, which makes it difficult to see exactly where to place the hook. The surface crochet is a simple form of tambour embroidery but worked with a crochet hook.

Materials: 200g Mohair Tweed (M): 100g Smoothie Tweed (C) (Thick bouclé mohair and acrylic): 100g Foxstones Lady (A): 7.00mm hook.

Size: To fit bust 86(95,102)cm (34(37,40)ins)

Tension: 9sts to 10cm (4in).

TO MAKE:

Work 38:43:47ch loosely in mohair yarn (the chain has to go round the back part of the hips and although there is a vent in the design, it should be loose).

Row 1: Work 1tr in 4th ch from hook, (do not count loop on hook) 1tr in each ch to end, 3ch, turn (36:41:45sts).

Row 2: 1tr in each tr to end, 1tr in turning chain, 3ch, turn.

Work row 2, 28 times.

Row 31: (divide for fronts) 1tr in each of next 11:13:15tr, 3ch, turn (12:14:16sts).

Row 32: As row 2—repeat this row 6 times.

Row 39: 1tr in each of next 10:12:14tr, 2tr in turning ch, 3ch, turn (13:15:17sts).

Work row 2, 3 times.

Rep rows 39–42 inclusive, twice (15:17:19sts).

Work row 2, 13 times.

Break off yarn.

Rejoin yarn at neck edge for the other front, leaving 12:13:13sts unworked.

Row 31a: 3ch, 11:13:15tr, 3ch, turn.

Work row 2, 7 times.

Row 39a: 1tr in same place as turning ch, 1tr in each st to end, 3ch, turn (13:15:17sts).

Work row 2, 3 times.

Rep the last 4 rows twice.

Work row 2, 13 times.

Fasten off.

Border (Armhole/Side Seams)

With RS facing and C yarn, work 1 row of dc placing 3dc across the ends of 2 treble rows, to central 5 rows of shoulder, 1dc in each row and of these 5 rows, 3dc to 3tr rows for the remaining length.

To work loop stitch insert hook into top of stitch and wrap yarn round first finger of left hand. Now put yarn round hook, and draw through one stitch. Yarn over hook, draw through 2sts, then work 1ch tightly to lock the loop into place. This ch is part of the loop stitch and does not count as a separate st. (See diagram 4.)

Next row: Join in yarns A and C and work them together. Place 1 loop st in each st to last 3sts, 3dc, 1ch, 2dc.

Row 3: 1ch, dc to central 4sts, (dc2tog) twice, dc to end.

Rep rows 2 and 3 once. Complete by working 1 row crab st on RS.

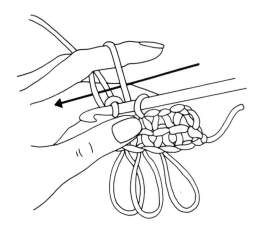

diagram 4

Front and Neck Border

With RS facing and A work dc up front using 4dc to 2tr row ends until back neck is reached dc2tog round corner of back neck, dc across neck, dc2tog at corner of back neck, dc down other front.
Next row: As row 2 of armhole.
Row 3: dc all round decreasing 1st at each corner of back neck.
Rep rows 2 and 3 once.
Complete by working 1 row crab st on RS.
Fasten off all ends.
Join side seams on wrong side with A yarn by leaving 30cm (12in) (ie 60cm (24in) armhole) and using dc to join—alternatively back st. The remaining stitches form a side vent.
Work motif in surface crochet as follows. (See diagram on page 18.) Have the yarn below the surface of the crochet on the wrong side using yarn A. With the hook inserted through the fabric from the right side, pick up yarn A and pull through to front. Insert the hook in a different place, to form a design. Make this part of your waistcoast individual and choose any design or idea you wish. Alternatively purchase a motif of embroidered satin or sequins and appliqué on.

PART FIVE
Challenging

VICTORIAN LACE

See page 74

The lace edgings on tablecloths in the Victorian era inspired this design. A larger hook and thicker cotton replace the fineness of the 'lace crochet'. A contrasting ribbon enhances the fashion detail, turning it into a collar rather than a tablecloth edging. Heavier cotton was used for the main work.

Materials: 350g Chanteleine Lea: 150g Chanteleine Fil d'Ecosse for collar: 5 metres narrow velvet ribbon: 5.50mm and 2.50mm crochet hooks.

Size: Medium (approx 87–92cm (34–36in). This size can be increased by multiples of 4 stitches on both back and front, to give extra shoulder length as well as a bigger bust size.

Tension: 6sts to 5cm (2in) in main yarn with 5.50mm hook.

TO MAKE:

Back:
With the thicker yarn and 5.50mm hook work 67ch (do not count the loop on the hook as a chain).
Row 1: 1tr in 4th ch from hook, 1tr in each ch to end, 2ch, turn. (65sts). This is the row which will have the tie threaded through at the end.
Row 2: *miss 1st, 1ch, 1dc in next st, rep from * to end, 1ch, turn (32 holes).
Row 3: *1dc in 1ch sp, 1dc in dc, rep from * to end, 2ch, turn
Note: when working into a ch sp, insert the hook into the hole and not the stitch.
Rep rows 2 and 3, 18 times **

Next row: ss over 4, work to last 4sts, turn.
Rep rows 3 and 2, 11 times. Break off yarn.

Do CHECK your stitches on the 'hole' row quite frequently as it is so easy to miss working the last stitch of the dc rows.

Note: Heavy cotton will drop with wear—please allow for this when making.

Front
Work as back to **
Next row ss over 3sts, 2ch, miss 1st, 1dc in next st, *1ch, miss 1st, 1dc in next st, rep from * 12 times (29sts).
Next row: 1ch, dc to end.
Work in pattern keeping the armhole edge straight and dec 1st at neck edge on next 16 rows (13sts).
Work 6 rows straight. Break off yarn.

2nd Neck Shaping
Rejoin yarn to 2nd st, 2ch, miss 1st, 1dc in next st *1ch, miss 1st, 1dc in next st, rep from * 12 times (29sts).
Next row: 1ch, dc to end.
Decrease 1st at neck edge on next 16 rows keeping armhole edge straight (13sts).
Work 6 rows straight. Break off yarn.
Join shoulders and sideseams with dc worked on wrong side.

Armholes
Work 2 rows dc making quite sure that not too many stitches have been used or it will frill.

Collar—Main Border
With thin cotton make 43ch using 2.50mm hook.
Row 1: 1tr in 7th ch from hook *1tr, miss 2ch, 2ch, rep from * to end (13sps) 6ch, turn.
Row 2: 1dc in 3rd ch from hook, 1htr, 10tr, (2ch, miss 2sts, 1tr) twice, 21tr, (2ch, 1tr on next tr) twice, 5ch, turn.
Row 3: 1tr on next tr *2ch, 1tr on tr, 3tr, rep from * 3 times, (2ch, 1tr on tr) 4 times, 6ch, turn.
Row 4: 1dc in 3rd ch from hook, 1htr, 10tr, (2ch, 1tr on next tr) twice, *3tr, 2ch, 1tr on tr 5 rep from * 3 times, 2ch, 1tr in last st, 3ch, turn.
Row 5: *(2ch, 1tr on tr) twice, 3tr, rep from * twice, (2ch, miss 2sts, 1tr) 4 times, 6ch, turn.
Row 6: As row 4.
Row 7: As row 3.
Row 8: As row 2.
Row 9: 1tr on tr, *2ch, miss 2sts, 1tr rep from * to end, 6ch, turn.
Rows 2–9 form the basic pattern. Repeat these 10 times.

Corner (for point of V-neck)
1dc in 3rd ch from hook, 1htr, 9tr, 3ch, turn, * miss 2sts, 1dc, 2ch, miss 2sts, 1tr, 6ch turn, 1dc in 3rd ch, 1htr, 8tr, 1htr, ss to last st, 3ch, turn. Rep from * 3 times but omitting tr and ss of last rep. Replace with 2tr, 2ch, join with ss to top of tr of last border row.
●ss in each of 2ch of border row and top of tr (2ch, miss 2sts, 1tr) 3

times, 6ch, turn. 1dc in 3rd ch from hook, 1htr, 10tr, 2ch ss to top of tr in border row. Rep from ●3 times. ss in each of 2ch and top of tr. (2ch, miss 2sts, 1tr) 3 times 6ch, turn.

Work Border pattern rows 2–9 incl until border fits neck loosely.

Join together first and last rows.

Run a gathering thread through collar.

Make SURE collar is pinned to neck line with both sides matching, and seam at centre back. Sew or double crochet collar to neck.

Thread velvet ribbon through both rows of holes at side of blocked squares. A third row of ribbon is threaded through one row of holes at other side of block square leaving the row nearest neck open.

PATCHWORK SHORTIE

See page 75

This is a pattern that is only the start of something that you can adapt to many other designs. The instructions are given for a three quarter sleeve, short length, aran-weight jacket. However as the patches are made to size, the yarn can be any thickness from 2-ply to rugwool. Simply change the size of the hook accordingly and work to size rather than stitches and rows.

- ☐ Add a width of patches to the sleeve to give full-length.
- ☐ Remove two widths of patches to make it short-sleeve.
- ☐ Remove 1 width of patches for an elbow length.
- ☐ Use the wrap over as a design feature on a sweater having the buttons on top of the overlap and omitting the buttonholes. This is excellent in a fine luxury yarn.
- ☐ Add more patches for added length to the 8 body widths. To avoid uncharacteristic straight line at waist level, be imaginative when piecing the patches together. Hip length or full length.
- ☐ Change from a 'coat of many colours' to a 'country-style' using the Special Breeds natural pure wool yarns as used for the jacket on page 38.
- ☐ Alternatively 'go bright, shed light!', especially for the younger generation, possibly using oddments from your own bit box.

Although this is a one-size jacket, again it is not difficult to take off 10cm (4in) or add multiples of 10cm (4in) to the width.

Do this by reducing or increasing the two strips that go over the shoulders by a multiple of 1.25cm ($\frac{1}{2}$in).

Materials: Forsell's Pure Wool Aran was used throughout.
8 shades were chosen. The whole was worked on a 5.50 crochet hook.
Yarn (A): Donkey 2 × 50g balls, Yarn (B): Ember 2 × 50g balls
Yarn (C): Khaki 2 × 50g balls, Yarn (D): Russett 4 × 50g balls
Yarn (E): Welsh Mountain 2 × 50g balls Yarn (F): Sage 2 × 50g balls
Yarn (G): Heather 2 × 50g balls Yarn (H): Cerise 2 × 50g balls

Size: To fit bust size 92cm (36in)

Tension: 10sts to 8cm (approx 3in)

TO MAKE:
Front Left hand Strip
12.5cm (5in) wide 81cm (32in) long.

Pattern
Make 19ch.
Row 1: 1tr in 4th ch from hook, 1tr in each st to end, 1ch turn (17sts).
Row 2: dc to end, 3ch, turn.
Row 3: tr to end, 1ch, turn.
Rows 2 and 3 form the pattern.
In pattern work 8 rows in all using yarn (A). Fasten off.
In pattern work 18 rows in all in yarn (F), fasten off.
In pattern work 28 rows in all in yarn (D), fasten off.
In pattern work 22 rows in all in yarn (G), fasten off.
Using yarn (D) join (G) to (D) then (D) to (F) and finally (F) to (A) by placing 2 pieces together so that the RS is on the outside. Crab stitch through both pieces to give a raised design line. Fasten off. Proceed to make all the strips first.

Centre back 38cm (15in) long
In pattern work 20 rows in (G), fasten off.
In pattern work 16 rows in (B), fasten off.
Join these 2 together with crab stitch in (D).

Centre Front 38cm (15in) long
Note: This is 2.5cm (1in) wider than the other strips to allow for the buttonholes and slight wrap over therefore work on 21sts.
In pattern work 10 rows in (H), fasten off.
In pattern work 5 rows in (E).
*On next row miss the 3rd st from RH edge when front of patch is facing, and replace with 1ch, (remember the turning ch IS a stitch)** then work 4 more rows. Fasten off. Join the START of this patch to the one just completed using yarn D and crab stitch.
In pattern, work 3 rows in (F).
Work from * to ** of last patch, work 7 rows in pattern work from *

to ** once, work 2 rows in pattern, fasten off. Join the start of this patch to the patch in yarn (H) making sure the buttonholes are in line.

Front Right Hand Strip
In pattern work 12 rows in all in yarn (A), fasten off.
In pattern work 14 rows in all in yarn (B), fasten off.
In pattern work 20 rows in all in yarn (C), fasten off.
In pattern work 12 rows in all in yarn (E), fasten off.
In pattern work 14 rows in all in yarn (B), fasten off.
Using yarn D and crab stitch, join (A) to (B), (B) to (C), (C) to (E) and (E) to (H).

Right Side Strip
20cm (8in) long 10cm (4in) wide
In pattern work 8 rows in (F), fasten off.
In pattern work 8 rows in (G), fasten off.
Join together with (D) and crab stitch.

Left Side Strip
In pattern work 4 rows in (B), fasten off.
In pattern work 12 rows in (A), fasten off.
Join together with (D) and crab stitch.

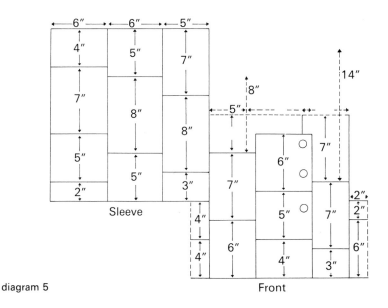

diagram 5

To complete Bodypiece
Place strips lengthway together as can be seen from photograph on page 75 and sketch above. Join with crab stitch in yarn (D) on right side of work, matching rows.

Right Sleeve 45cm (18in) round sleeve
The first strip nearest the armholes is the same width as the body strips.

Work 6 rows pattern in (A), fasten off.
Work 16 rows pattern in (B), fasten off.
Work 18 rows pattern in (C), fasten off.
Using (D) join (A) to (B) and (B) to (C) in crab stitch on right side of work. Join just 7.5cm (3in) of (A) to (C) to form a tube. Continue to connect the remaining 5cm (2in) to (G) of the Right Side strip. Then connect the armhole to the first sleeve strip with yarn D and crab stitch on right side of work.

Second Strip 15cm (6in) wide (therefore using 20sts).
Work 18 rows pattern in (D), fasten off.
Work 22 rows pattern in (E), fasten off.
Join together with (D) on RS in crab stitch to form a tube.
Join this tube with (D) to the sleeve section already connected.

Third Strip 15cm (6in) wide
Work 12 rows pattern in (F), fasten off.
Work 16 rows pattern in (G), fasten off.
Work 12 rows pattern in (H), fasten off.
Join (F) to (G) and (G) to (H) using (D) on RS in crab stitch. Join (H) to (F) to form a tube. Join this tube to the sleeve.

Sleeve Edge
In (D) with 5.00mm hook, and RS facing work 1 row dc round edge of sleeve.
Final row: Work 1 row crab stitch.

Left Sleeve

First Strip
Work as 3rd strip of right sleeve but divide the 12 rows of (F) into 2 pieces of 6 rows (for underarm join).
Complete in the same way as first sleeve with 2nd strip identical to right sleeve and the 3rd strip in the same patches as the first strip.

To Finish
Commence at centre back neck with yarn (D) and 5.00mm hook.
Have RS facing and work 1 row dc round neck, fronts, base of jacket, back to centre neck. Remember to decrease one stitch at each of the 3 inside corners of the neck and to increase at the right angle corners at the base of jacket and neck overlap.
Final row: crab stitch to end.
Fasten off all ends and sew buttons on to match.

POLESTAR COAT

See page 82

An interesting use of different stitches and pure wool 'Special Breed Fleeces', this coat is an excellent design to lengthen into a full-length coat. To create a good 'swing' while walking, insert long but narrow isosceles triangles from waist to hem crocheted from Jacobs yarn. These will also enhance the finished article.

Materials: 150g Forsell's Pure Wool Aran: 100g Forsell's Pure Wool Suffolk: 200g Forsell's Pure Wool Cheviot: *150g Forsell's Pure Wool Jacobs: 100g Forsell's Pure Wool Welsh Mountain: 6.00mm and 5.50mm crochet hooks. 56cm (22in) Zip.
*If the jacket is to be enlarged, use the Jacobs yarn to increase the width of the shoulder strip and the underarm triangle.

Size: To fit approx 90cm (35in) bust, but width of strip 4 can be adjusted in width to fit any size.

Tension: 5sts = 4cm ($1\frac{1}{2}$in). Note: It is important that the width of the strips are correct or the jacket will be a different size.

TO MAKE:
See diagram 6 for position of strips.

Strip 1(a) in Suffolk. 2 alike for each side of zip.
With 6.00mm hook make 8ch, 1dc in 4th ch from hook, *1tr, 1dc rep from * to end (6sts) 3ch, turn.
Row 2: *1dc on tr, 1tr on dc, rep to last st, 1dc in last st.
Work row 2 until 56cm (22in) have been worked.
Make another strip the same.

Strip 1(b)
Work another strip in the same stitch, still with Suffolk yarn but using 10sts (i.e. 12ch to start).
Length of this centre back strip is 61cm (24in).

Strip 2(a) in Cheviot
On 6.00mm hook make 10ch,
Row 1: 1tr in 4th ch from hook, 1tr in each ch to end, (8sts).
Row 2: 2ch turn, 1 raised treble front, *2RtrB, 2RtrF, rep from * to end, 2ch turn.
Rep this row until 61cm (24in) have been reached.
Work another strip the same.

Strip 2(b)
Work as strip 2a until 56cm (22in) has been worked.

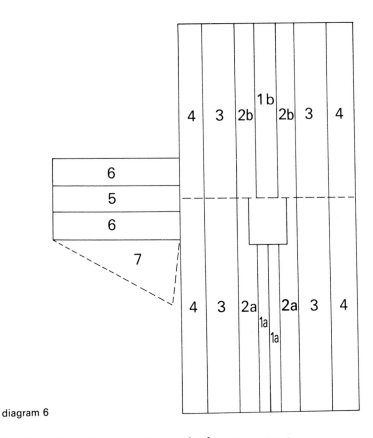

diagram 6

Continue in pattern on 4sts only for 10cm (4in).
Work another strip the same.

Strip 3 in Welsh Mountain Black with Aran.
With 6.00mm hook and dark, make 20ch to form 18sts.
This strip is Polish Star Stitch which uses an extended treble (Etr) to give height to plait the chain loops.
The chain loops are NOT counted as working sts.
Commence work in extended treble as though working an ordinary treble. There is an additional operation at the beginning of the stitch as follows: yoh, insert hook under 2 strands of next st, yoh, pull through to front (3 loops on hook), yoh, pull through 1 loop (still 3 loops on hook), (yoh pull through 2 loops) twice—an extended treble made. Make 2 strips 66cm (26in) and 2, 57cm (22in).

Polish Star Stitch
This is based on a multiple of 8sts using an extended treble as given above. The 10 chain loops between the groups of stitches are interlocked before the final row is worked. 2 tones or 2 colours give the best effect.
With colour A make 20ch. (See detail photograph on page 79).
Row 1: In A 1Etr in 4th ch from hook, 10ch, *miss 1ch, 1Etr in next 4ch, 10ch, miss 1ch, (2Etr in next ch) twice, 10ch, rep from * twice, 4Etr, 10ch, miss 1ch, 2Etr in last ch.
Row 2: In B 3ch, turn, 2Etr in next tr, 10ch, *miss 1tr, 2Etr, 10ch,

miss 1tr, 2Etr in next tr, 2Etr, 2Etr in next st, 10ch, rep from * twice, miss 1tr, 2Etr, 10ch, miss 1tr, 2Etr in next tr, 1Etr in turning ch. DO NOT TURN WORK.

Row 3: In A 3ch to turn on top of turning ch of row 2, 1Etr, 10ch, *miss 1tr, (2Etr in next st) twice, 10ch, miss 1tr, 4Etr, 10ch, rep from * twice, miss 1tr, (2Etr in next tr) twice, 10ch, miss 1tr, 2Etr.

Row 4: In B 13ch, miss 1tr, *2Etr in next tr, 2Etr, 2Etr in next tr, 10ch, miss 1tr, 2Etr, 10ch, miss 1tr, rep from * twice, 2Etr in next tr, 2Etr, 2Etr in next tr, 10ch, 1Etr in last set. DO NOT TURN WORK.

Row 5: In A 3ch on top of turning ch, 1Etr in same place, 10ch, *miss 1tr, 4Etr, 10ch, miss 1tr, (2Etr in next tr) twice, 10ch, rep from *twice, miss 1tr, Etr, 10ch, miss 1tr, 2Etr in last tr.

Rows 2–5 incl form the basic pattern.

When work is long enough, work a final row with A after the loops have been interlinked (see diagram 7).

diagram 7

Interlink Stages:

1. Thread RH loop through LH loop where loops are closest. These crossed loops will lie over colour strip B.
2. Thread colour B through loop A using the nearest B loop lying on the same diagonal line as stage 1.
3. Thread colour A through B keeping the diagonal line.
4. Cross colour A by threading the RH side through the LH side.

Repeat stages 2–4 inclusive to top of crochet.

The chains worked between the trebles of the Polish Star Stitch need to be linked as shown, so that the loose fabric closes into a regular textile weight and design.

Final row: In A work 4Etr in centre 4 of the 6Etr in previous row. Work 1dc in 10ch loop. Work 4Etr in 2Etr in previous row.

Work 2 strips 61cm (24in) in length

Work 2 strips 66cm (26in) in length

Strip 4 in Jacobs yarn

(This can be widened by a multiple of 2sts).

With 6.00mm crochet hook make 7ch.

Row 1: 1tr in 4th ch from hook, 1tr in each ch to end, 1ch turn (5sts).

Row 2: *1dtr, 1dc rep from * to end, 3ch turn.

Row 3: tr to end, 1ch, turn.
Rep rows 2 and 3 until 61cm (24in) has been reached.
Make another strip the same.
Work 2 further strips for the front to measure 66cm (26in).

Strip 5 in Aran
With 6.00mm hook make 15ch.
Row 1: 1tr in 4th ch from hook, tr to end, 3ch, turn.
Row 2: 2tr, 1 popcorn (see Sweater page 48) 5tr, 1 popcorn 3tr, 3ch, turn.
Row 3: tr to end, 3ch, turn.
Row 4: 5tr, 1 popcorn, 6tr, 3ch, turn.
Row 5: As row 3.
Repeat the last 4 rows until 41cm (16in) has been reached.
Work another strip to match.

Strip 6 in Cheviot
With 6.00mm hook make 12ch.
Row 1: 2tr in 3rd ch from hook, miss 2ch, 1dc in next ch, miss 2ch, 5tr in next ch, miss 2ch, 1dc in last ch.
Row 2: 3ch, 2tr in same place, 1dc in centre of 5tr, 5tr in dc, 1dc in last st.
Rep row 2 until 41cm (16in) has been made.
Make a further 3 strips the same.

Strip 7 in Jacobs
Technically this is a triangle.
With 6.00mm hook, 3ch, 2tr in same place as turning ch, 1ch, turn.
Row 2: dc to end, 3ch, turn.
Row 3: 1tr in same place as turning ch, tr to last st, 2tr in last st, 1ch 5 turn.
Rep these two rows until 39sts (19tr rows) have been worked.
Finish with a dc row.
Work another piece the same.

Make up
Carefully safety pin all strips together.
Join shoulder seam strips on the wrong side using the same yarn as that worked in the strip.
Join all long strips together down their full length with the right sides on the outside. Use the 5.50mm hook to work crab st along the length. Work Aran crab stitch down the zip side of strip, 1 join strips 1 and 2 with Aran. Join strips 2 to 3 with Welsh Mountain Black. Join strips 3 to 4 with Welsh Mountain Black. Join the top of the sleeves and underarm seam on the wrong side with Jacobs. Join strip 5 to 6 using Welsh Mountain Black on the right side in crab stitch.
Join strip 6 to 7 on the right side using Aran and crab stitch.

Cuff
With 5.00mm hook and Cheviot yarn work 3 rows of dc and 1 row of crab st.
Fasten off.

Neck
With 5.00mm hook and Cheviot yarn work 5 rows dc decreasing 2 tog at 4 inside corners of neck. Complete neck with 1 row of crab stitch. Finally insert zip being very careful that the zip lies absolutely flat and does not buckle.

LANDSCAPE WAISTCOAT

See page 83

This is a pattern for experienced crochet workers only. It is based on a graph and will involve an interesting search for the yarns before you begin. These will possibly be found among your own remnants and oddments of yarn. A variety of interesting yarns that have a texture and a multi-dyed effect is what you are looking for. The yarns can be collected from an ordinary woolshop, or can be remnants on cones from a millshop, or can come from craft shops and from embroidery threads. Basically you are looking for lightweight mohair, and/ or brushed acrylic with mohair, and/or brushed wool. Some of the yarns should have quite surprising slubs, 'rag-tail', or knops.

The yarns that have been used in the example given are shown on page 86 as a guide.

TO MAKE

Stage 1: Draw out the waistcoat pattern, see diagram 8 (this was to fit a size 34in (85cm) bust) enlarge for size 38in (96cm) by adding 2in (5cm) from the shoulders round, as per the dotted line on the pattern. This will give more garment at the fronts to cover the bust.

Stage 2: Carefully transfer the lines indicating the blocks of colour on to your paper pattern. You now have an actual size paper pattern with the basic landscape blocks drawn on.

Stage 3: Keeping the paper pattern flat at all times on a table, and working the crochet to the pattern, proceed with yarn (A).

Stage 4: Using a number 6.00mm hook work yarn (A) in such a way that you are increasing and decreasing to create a scalloped shape. Continue this scalloped shaping until a piece of crochet exactly as (A) shown on the graph is completed.

Stage 5: Use yarn (B) to work on to the block of crochet already made, finishing at the point below (H) and at the side of (F). Place

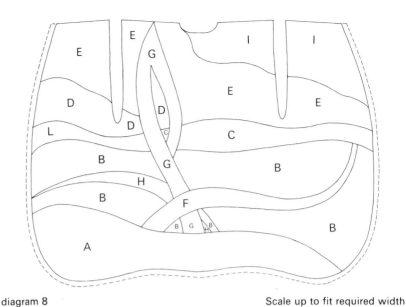

diagram 8   Scale up to fit required width

yarn (F) next to yarn (B) linking the tops of the rows into the edges of the rows of block B. The easiest way to link is to remove your hook from the loop, insert it into the crochet at the side of the work and pull it through. Work your turning chain and connect the chain into the top of the next row. Now proceed as though you were working an ordinary row. Turn at the end and come back along the row connecting once more.

Stage 6: Continue working the blocks of colour from the base upwards, breaking off the yarns as one block is completed.
Note: Do not try to work up a front or even up the left side of the back before completing the body measurements, as this is an easy way to get distortion.
Helpful hint: One way to keep the work flat is constantly to lay the crochet on the actual paper pattern and whenever fullness appears to be occurring, work a decrease at that point on the next row. Similarly, if the work is pulling in slightly, away from the lines on the pattern depicting colour blocks, add a stitch.

Stage 7: Having reached the armholes work up the front, then the back and finally the second front (see picture as an additional aid). Whenever possible do not change your hook size. This is one of the controlling factors. If you look at the swatches you will see that the weight of yarns are similar. Only the machine knitting yarns are thinner but they are used double. This is only possible because there is a balance in yarns (H) and (F) that give equal weight within the waistcoat; and yarn (G) runs as a narrow column up the back. The use of these yarns which are heavier than the rest of the yarns in the waistcoat can be achieved successfully if a balance of weight is considered.

Stage 8: Join the shoulders. Unless you particularly want to 'frame' your picture with a dark colour I would advise against edging the waistcoat, either at the front and base or at the armholes.

Stage 9: Surface work can now be carefully added. Again if you look at the picture you will note that most of the surface work has gone over one shoulder. This is to prevent the weight of the yarn being used for the surface crochet, pulling against the lighter weight mohairs on which it is worked. The green bouclé yarn has had only small quantities scattered along the length of yarn (F). Here again, because the waistcoat is not lined, it is *very* important that the weight of yarn used for the surface crochet does not pull the pattern and design out of shape.

The beauty of this particular pattern is that it is 'no pattern'. The crochet worker has to 'play' with the yarns and the shapes and use her skills and knowledge to make the whole lie flat and in shape. Another interesting thing about this particular pattern is that any season of the year can be depicted, so if you have not succeeded in getting the yarns in the photograph, then you can go for a summer or winter scene using whatever yarns you have available.

TECHNIQUES

This section is a guide to achieving crochet that looks good, wears well and launders well. There is no one right way to do anything in crochet, but there are good ways and bad ways. If the method you are using in your crochet gives you an inaccurate tension, falls apart at joins or seams, and generally has that 'home-made' look, then try some of the techniques that are briefly outlined below.

THE HOOK

When working with small hooks that have the stiletto shape (that is the old embroidery style of hook which has carried through in some steel hooks) it is necessary to make absolutely sure that the loops being worked do not come very far up the stem of the crochet hook itself or the tension will get looser. The further along the stem the loop has to travel, the larger the circumference, by the very nature of the shape of the hook. With the medium range hooks, approximately 2.00mm to 5.00mm (see Hook Sizes page 6), the place to hold the hook is either at the point where the plastic handle joins the metal crochet rod, or the flat part of the crochet stem in the unhandled crochet hooks. Larger hooks should be held further down the stem, away from the hook. The idea of using a large hook is to create a looser fabric. If the hook is held too close to the hook head, the loop being made cannot travel easily on to the regular part of the stem. When the hook is held lower down all the loops will travel on to the correct circumference of the hook.

HOLDING THE YARN

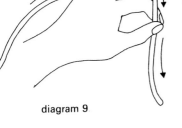

diagram 9

How you hold the yarn really does not matter as long as the tension achieved is correct. Some people find they get cramp in their little finger, or find their shoulder and elbow rather painful after crocheting for a long time. Should this happen to you, it would be advisable for you to try holding the yarn as shown in diagram 9. This carries the yarn round two fingers instead of one thus eliminating the tendency to grip the yarn with the little finger. Simply have the palm of the hand face down, bring the yarn from the palm to the back of the hand between the middle and ring fingers, take it over the little and ring fingers, and once more bring it from the palm to the back of the hand. This creates just sufficient tension to keep it taut during crochet without the fingers actually gripping the yarn. Continue bringing the yarn over the middle and index finger which, if spread apart will form a bridge which will allow the hook head to be inserted under the yarn for easy use.

SLIP KNOT

The following method of making a slip knot is very useful should you decide to make your own buttons, or require circles which have a tightly worked centre rather than a hole. This method allows the tail end of the yarn to be pulled up after the first chain has been worked into, thus making it possible to draw the thread tight and so eliminate the gap in the centre of the circle.

To make a slip knot, cross the tail end of the yarn over the main length coming from the ball or cone and form a loop. Continue taking this end over and behind the loop just made. Insert the hook under the single thread that has materialized as shown in diagram 10. Now tighten the slip knot onto the hook by nipping the thread from the ball and the tail end and pulling the hook upwards. At this stage the loop rarely fits snugly onto the hook so pull the tail, thus tightening it to the correct size.

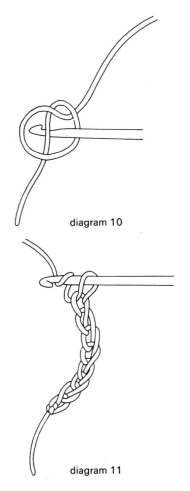
diagram 10

diagram 11

CHAIN

1. First make a slip knot.
2. Put the yarn over the hook as shown in diagram 11 and pull through the loop already on the hook. (1 chain (ch) made).

Chains are used when turning the work in order to raise the hook to the height required for the next row of the pattern. They are used as foundation chains into which subsequent stitches can be placed. Chains can also be used to achieve lacy patterns.

SLIP STITCH

A slip stitch is simply a chain that has been connected to the work. Insert the hook into the work, put the yarn over the hook (yoh) picking up two strands as normal, and draw the thread through all the loops on the hook (one slip stitch (ss) made). See diagram 12.

Slip stitches are used to connect rows of work when working circles or tubes, thus making them rounds (rnd) see diagram 13. They are also used to carry the yarn over stitches which are no longer needed in the work. Slip stitches do not have any height and therefore are useful when taking the yarn over short distances. A third use for a slip stitch is as a connecting stitch within crochet fabric patterns.

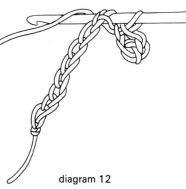
diagram 12

INSERTING HOOK

Unless your pattern actually tells you differently, the hook is placed under the top two threads that give a chain–like appearance on the top of the stitch. The hook is placed fractionally to one side of the stitch in order to do this. For this reason it is recommended that work is turned on every row or round, to avoid a bias occurring in the seam.

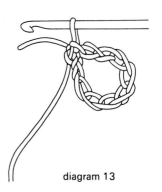
diagram 13

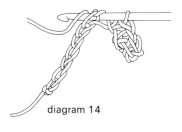

diagram 14

DOUBLE CROCHET (dc) 1ch TO TURN

To make a double crochet insert the hook into the work from front to back picking up two strands (as shown in diagram 14), yarn over hook, draw this yarn to the front of the work but not through the loop originally on the hook. There are now two loops on the hook. Yarn over hook once more and draw through the two loops (1double crochet made) see diagram 15. The height of a double crochet is not great, so at the end of the row only one chain is needed before turning the work.

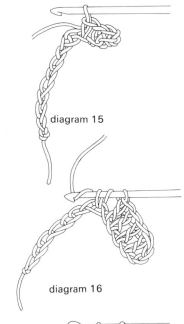

diagram 15

diagram 16

TURNING WORK AT THE END OF A ROW

As chains have a smooth and a rough side it is recommended that any turning chain be made before the work is turned, then turn the work away from you (not towards you like the page of a book if you are a right handed crocheter). Once this work is turned the chain just made represents the first stitch of the row. Insert the hook into the next stitch which should not be the same place as the turning chain, unless an increase is required.

TREBLE (tr) 3ch TO TURN

To make a treble put yarn over hook before inserting into the stitch, by picking up two strands as normal, yarn over hook and draw this through to the front of the work giving three loops on the hook. Yarn over hook again and draw through two of the loops on the hook, leaving two loops remaining. Place the yarn over hook once more and draw through the last two loops. All crochet begins and ends with one loop on the hook no matter how complicated the process. At the end of the row, three chains are required to lift the hook to the height of the next treble row. Some crochet workers have got into the habit of making their chains pleasantly loose and might require only two chains to turn. See diagrams 16 and 17.

diagram 17

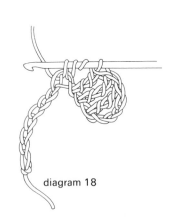

diagram 18

DOUBLE TREBLES (dtr) 4 CHAIN TO TURN

A double treble requires the yarn to be wrapped round the hook twice before insertion into the work. Yarn round hook and pull through to the front, giving four loops on the hook *yarn round hook and draw through two loops, rep from * twice to leave one loop on the hook (1 double treble made). See diagram 18.

TRIPLE TREBLES (tr tr) 5 CHAIN TO TURN

To make a triple treble wrap the yarn round the hook 3 times and insert into the wool in the usual way. Wrap the yarn over the hook and draw to the front of the work giving five loops on the hook. *Yoh and draw through two loops, rep from * 3 times (1tr tr made). See diagram 19.

QUADRUPLE TREBLES (quad tr) 6 CHAIN TO TURN

To make quadruple trebles wrap the yarn round the hook four times and insert into the works in the usual way. Yarn over hook and draw the thread to the front leaving six loops on the hook. *yoh and draw through two loops, rep from * 4 times (1quad tr made) See diagram 20.

The last three stitches are often referred to as long trebles. The stitch below is a short treble.

HALF TREBLE (htr) 2 CHAIN TO TURN

The half treble has a different appearance when finished than other basic stitches. This is because it has three strands giving a double chain look, unlike the two strands which form the single chain look of most stitches. Yarn over hook and insert into work in the normal way. Yarn over hook and pull through to the front. Yarn over hook and draw through all three loops on the hook. (1htr made) See diagram 21.

Note: You may find it advisable to insert the hook at the start of the row in the same place as the turning chain commences. Omit working into the turning chain at the end of the row.

CRAB STITCH

Sometimes referred to as Corded edge, Rope stitch, Russian stitch, Shrimp stitch and Reversed double crochet.

This stitch is worked from left to right (if you are right handed) unlike the normal working from right to left. The stitch is nearly always used as a finishing row or edging and is more pronounced when the right side is facing. Insert the hook into the next stitch on the right (left handed workers on the left) picking up two strands as normal. Drop the hook onto the yarn behind the work, rather than trying to pick it up in the normal way, and bring the thread through to the front by tilting the hook upwards so that two strands are on the hook. Twist the hook back to its normal working position, yarn over hook, and pull through the two loops on the hook so that there is only one loop remaining. See diagram 22.

INCREASING

Increasing is simple in crochet—it requires two stitches to be put in the place where one stitch is normally made. However in very thick yarn this will leave a hole. Insert the hook under one strand (ie say front loop) for the first stitch, and then insert the hook through the remaining strand (ie the back loop) for the second stitch. This will make the stitch less noticeable.

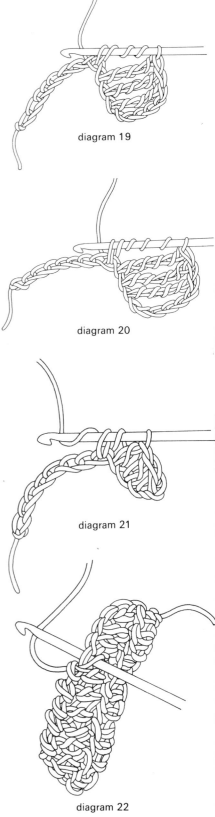

diagram 19

diagram 20

diagram 21

diagram 22

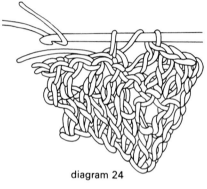

diagram 23

DECREASING

For most stitches the method of decreasing is to use two stitches that are then drawn together at the top so that there is only one chain loop to work into on the way back. To do this work the first stitch as usual but do not complete it, instead stop when two loops still remain on the hook. Now work the second stitch until there are three loops on the hook, yarn over hook, and draw through all three loops. This method of decreasing does not leave holes or create steps. See diagram 23 which uses the treble to illustrate the decrease.

FASTENING OFF

After the final stitch has been worked break the yarn from the main ball leaving approximately 15cm (6in), or more if you wish to use the yarn to complete a join. Work one chain with this piece of yarn but continue to pull it straight through the loop so that a little knot is formed. Slide the finger and thumb down so that the knot tightens close to the work.

JOINING YARNS

There are many different methods of joining yarn into the work. One join that is not easily felt, seen, and which will withstand wear and tear, is given below.

During working, the yarn will be at the top of a stitch in a row once the stitch is completed. However in a solid fabric a neat way to join a new ball of yarn is to commence working the next stitch drawing the yarn through to the front. See diagram 24. There should be approximately 10cm (4in) remaining at this stage. Complete the stitch with the new yarn. Remove the loop from the hook and proceed to insert it into the back loop of the next stitch. Draw the two ends of the yarn through the back loop of that stitch (there are no loops on the hook at this moment in time) *insert hook into the next stitch along through the back loop and draw the two strands through, repeat from * until all the yarn has been used. This creates a whipped look over the back loops of the stitches. Return to the working loop and now continue along the row inserting the hook in the normal way under two strands (unless the pattern specifies different) thus working over the ends of the yarn and trapping them even more tightly into the fabric. There are of course other ways of joining. The one described here is not suitable for lacy fabrics.

Long threads can be left in lacy fabrics and a sewing needle used to fasten these in to the work invisibly at the end. Alternatively if the yarn being used will allow it, one thread can be darned into the other as shown in diagram 25.

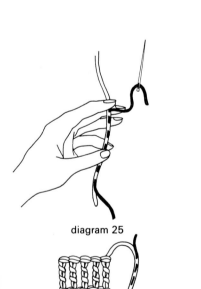

diagram 24

diagram 25

SURFACE CROCHET (TAMBOUR METHOD)

The main thing to remember when working surface chain on crochet fabrics is to ensure that this surface crochet is sufficiently loose for it to have the same elasticity and flexibility as the fabric onto which the chain is being worked. At the same time care must be taken not to over compensate for flexibility as this will make the surface chain loose which can be displeasing to the eye and can be caught on protruding obstacles during wear. See page 18.

SURFACE CROCHET (YARN ON TOP)

This method of surface crochet is worked by having the yarn on top of the fabric. The hook is inserted from above as in the tambour method, but the fabric is 'pinched' so that a hole stem of a crochet stitch, or a few fibres of woven cloth, can be used to anchor the crochet and hook emerges still on the right side of the fabric. A crocheted fabric can be made with surface crochet in mind. Raised treble or double treble ridges being a good example.

JOINING IN A DIFFERENT COLOURED YARN

If a new colour is joined in after a stitch has been fully completed, there is a colour drag. The loop on the hook becomes part of the next stitch. This means that at the end of a row the bottom chain of the series of chains needed to lift the hook to the required height is in the old colour. To avoid a 'colour drag', do not complete the last stitch of the row below. At the point where there are two loops remaining on the hook, wrap the new yarn over the hook and complete the stitch with the new yarn. Proceed with the new yarn from this point.

JOINING SEAMS

Once more there are many ways to join seams. On the whole the patterns in this book have eliminated seams wherever possible. Because of the height of the various stitches and the texture created by the crochet, joining seams has to be very carefully done if they are not to be visible. The methods given below are just some ways of joining seams—the choice is yours. However, some points have been included to help you decide which method to use in which article.

1. Double crochet the seams together on the wrong side of the work (that is with the right side of the fabric facing each other). The use of a double crochet as a join allows the work to drop if the laundering is not particularly good or if the yarns are heavy and the crochet fabric fairly loose. Wherever there is tendency for the crochet to 'drop', a double crochet join will 'drop' with it.

2. Crab stitch can be used to join pieces together on the right side of the work (that is with the wrong side of the crochet fabric facing each other). This is a particularly good method where design lines and/or texture is required. It will 'drop' in wear if necessary, in exactly the same way as a double crochet.

3. In lacy patterns a faggoting style join is suitable. That is to work three chains from one piece of work across the seam opening to join with a slip stitch into the other piece of work. Crochet three chains and anchor with a slip stitch into the first piece of crochet. Although this is a particularly good join for

any lacy fabrics it must be pointed out that it increases the width of the work as it is not closing the seam together but connecting it with an open join. This extra width must be taken into account for size.

4. Sew seams with a back stitch. This is quite adequate for many joins, particularly where the yarn is firm and ungiving. In a soft yarn or a looser crochet fabric, the back stitch will probably not give or drop in the same way as the double crochet or crab stitch and the resulting seam will become uneven after wear or use.

5. An oversewing stitch can be used giving a flat look. This is particularly useful where coloured stripes or bands have been included in the crochet. Where there are many different changes of colour it is often difficult to crochet the seams together and an alternative is the oversewing or flat stitch.

This is by no means the full list of methods to join seams but there should be sufficient information given to enable you to give a professional look to your work.

WORKING A TENSION SQUARE

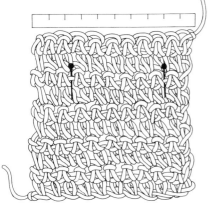

diagram 26

Work a sufficiently large square of crochet in the stitch that has been given under the heading tension. This square should be at least four stitches and four rows larger than the number of stitches given in the tension check. If you make a tension to exactly the number of stitches given in the pattern then you do not have a true guide. The rows at the commencement of the work can either be too tight or too slack and therefore should not be included in your tension check. Similarly the turning chains at the end of the row can again be either too tight or too slack, thus distorting the actual tension of the whole. Diagram 26 shows how and where to place the pins that will be required to mark the beginning and end of the stitches given in the tension check pattern. These pins should be inserted either in the centre of the stitch, or in the centre of the space between stitches. The distance between the two pins is then measured accurately.

Note: If you have had your tape measure a long time it may be worthwhile investing in a new one. Fabric tape measures eventually fray and plastic tape measures can strangely (despite many improved production methods) stretch in use. If your tension check gives you the number of rows, required to a certain measure, count these in the normal way but still please check that you are starting and ending your counting at the same point of a row.

BLOCK PRESSING

In general, pressing crochet is a much debated subject. Again there are no strict rules but the following guidelines have been found to work quite well for all yarns with the exception of cotton and linen.

1. Do not press work if surface or raised stitches are incorporated.
2. Be very wary of pressing acrylic with a damp cloth as this causes the yarn to stretch.

3. Only lightly press background fabrics, e.g. double crochets, trebles, etc.

To block press, pin the work onto a blanket starting from the centre of each side' or from four quarters of a circle. Have the pinheads nestling into the blanket and not the work. Continue to pin on each side working in opposite pairs see diagram 27. With a damp cloth cover the pinned-out article. Use a hot iron and press over the cloth. Do not move the iron, just press firmly. When each part of the article has been pressed, remove the cloth and lightly iron. Leave the crochet pinned out until completely dry when it can be removed from the blanket.

Note: A cotton cloth is best for pressing.

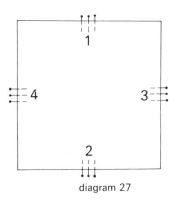

diagram 27

PRESSING

Do not press any work unless your pattern tells you to.

READING THE PATTERN

People do find reading a crochet pattern a little more difficult than reading a knitting pattern, or any other craft instruction. Possibly the reason for this is that most people are unaware that in crochet it is necessary to read a pattern from one comma to the next comma as one instruction. Everything between the two commas is one crochet process. Sometimes this can be quite long particularly in lacy patterns. For instance an instruction can be 2 trebles 1 chain 1 treble 2 chain 1 treble 1 chain 3 trebles in the next 2 chain space. The chain space being the key to where to put the stitches.

RAISED TREBLE RIB (see diagram 28)

Commence on a foundation chain which should be the inside edge of the rib, not the cuff, neck or welt edge. The chain does not stretch, the raised trebles do.

Work 1 row trebles.

Row 2: 2ch, *(yoh, insert hook from R to L round stem of tr st of row blow, yoh, draw to front—3 loops on hook—now work as a tr); this is 1 raised treble at front (1RtrF), (yoh, insert hook from R to L round stem of tr st but inserting hook from back to front, yoh, draw loop onto hook to give 3 loops—now work as a tr)—this is 1 raised treble at back (1RtrB), rep from * to end, 2ch, turn.

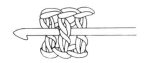

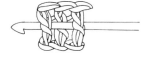

diagram 28

Note: The stitches are being pushed alternately back and forwards and should be kept in unbroken rows as in a knitted rib, until the cuff is completed.

LAUNDRY AND AFTER CARE

Rarely does crochet need to be dry-cleaned. If in doubt, wash the article in a cold water wash, either by hand or machine.

Remove excess water by (a) placing item in a white terry towel and allowing the excess moisture to be absorbed by the towel or (b) if washing by machine, place on a short spin.

Complete the drying by leaving the article flat. DO NOT tumble dry unless you are 100% sure of the outcome.

If the fabric is open and lacy, you may find washing the article in a white pillowcase an advantage as this will prevent any loops getting caught.

Avoid hanging crochet garments when storing.

In dry central heating atmospheres the yarns will dry out. Do not be afraid to allow the natural atmospheric moisture to be absorbed back into them.

SUPPLIES

All supplies within this book should be available at large wool stores. However smaller towns may not have yarn shops that supply the larger hooks and some of the more unusual yarns. All supplies can be obtained from the Crochet Design Centre, White Cross, South Road, Lancaster LA1 4XH should you be experiencing difficulty locally. The use of small amounts of Forsell Aran in two of the designs can also be obtained by post from the Crochet Design Centre.

ACKNOWLEDGEMENTS

I would like to express my thanks to the following people who pulled out 'all-the-stops' to help me complete this book on time. Crocheters: Carol, Dorothy, Gwen, Molly, Pamela, Pat, Rita and Tracey. Pattern/Yarn suppliers: Chriss of Avocet, Kay of Coats, Mike of Forsells, Mike of Foxstones, Thelma of Smallwares and Mr. Gordon Warwick of Sirdar. A special thanks to Catherine who tested a beginners pattern, typed the manuscript and attempted to keep me sane. And also Jane Elliot for her co-operation which made it easier for me.

The publishers would like to acknowledge Fenwicks and C&A for kindly supplying the additional clothes and accessories used throughout the book. They also wish to thank the photographer, Steve Tanner and stylist, Sue Duffy, for their untiring work behind the camera.